CLEP® PRINCIPLES OF MACROECONOMICS

Richard Sattora, M.S.
Blue Ribbon Teacher of Economics (Federal Reserve Bank of Dallas)

Research & Education Association
Visit our website at: www.rea.com

Research & Education Association
61 Ethel Road West
Piscataway, New Jersey 08854
E-mail: info@rea.com

**CLEP® Principles of Macroeconomics
with Online Practice Exams**

Published 2018
Copyright © 2013 by Research & Education Association, Inc.
Prior edition copyright © 2008 by Research & Education
Association, Inc. All rights reserved. No part of this book may
be reproduced in any form without permission of the publisher.

Printed in the United States of America

Library of Congress Control Number: 2012945549

ISBN-13: 978-0-7386-1088-7
ISBN-10: 0-7386-1088-7

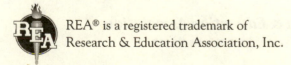

CONTENTS

CHAPTER 3

ABOUT THE AUTHOR

Richard Sattora is an AP Economics teacher at Excelsior Award-winning Pittsford Mendon High School, Pittsford, N.Y., where he has taught for 30 years. The caliber of his work has brought Mr. Sattora recognition from *Who's Who Among America's Teachers* and the Federal Reserve Bank of Dallas, which named him a Blue Ribbon Teacher of Economics.

In 2005, under Mr. Sattora's direction, Pittsford Mendon High School's Federal Reserve Challenge Team won the Fed Challenge national championship. This prestigious national economics competition is sponsored by the Board of Governors of the Federal Reserve System and promotes a greater understanding of economics among students. Mr. Sattora has also designed an Economic Education Institute blueprint for the Federal Reserve Bank of New York. A graduate of Canisius College, he holds an M.S. degree from Nazareth College.

Mr. Sattora's varied background in economics gives him a balanced perspective on the subject. He has worked for Eastman Kodak Co. and been involved in many entrepreneurial activities in the real estate, restaurant, and landscaping fields. He is a member of the Rochester Area Council of Social Studies and the Association of Private Enterprise Educators.

AUTHOR ACKNOWLEDGMENTS

I extend special thanks to my wife, Jeanette, and my sons, Jeffrey and Christopher, without whose patience and support this work could not have been completed. I would also like to acknowledge my parents, Howard and Betty, for the special role they played in all of my accomplishments. I am grateful to the former and current staff of the Federal Reserve Bank of Dallas, especially Wayne Hast, whose generosity and support for high school economics teachers allowed me to attend my first APEE conference that began this journey. I also thank other members of the Federal Reserve Bank of Dallas including former President Bob McTeer, Chief Economist C. Michael Cox, and economist Bob Formiani whose presentations and writings continue to educate and inspire me. Finally, I would like to thank the staff of the Federal Reserve Branch Bank of Buffalo, economist Richard Dietz, Kausar Hamdani, and Diana Bley for their support of my Federal Reserve Challenge Team.

— Richard Sattora

ABOUT REA

Founded in 1959, Research & Education Association (REA) is dedicated to publishing the finest and most effective educational materials—including study guides and test preps—for students of all ages. Today, REA's wide-ranging catalog is a leading resource for students, teachers, and other professionals. Visit *www.rea.com* to see a complete listing of all our titles.

PUBLISHER ACKNOWLEDGMENTS

We would like to thank Pam Weston, Publisher, for setting the quality standards for production integrity and managing the publication to completion; John Paul Cording, Vice President, Technology, for coordinating the design and development of the REA Study Center; Larry B. Kling, Vice President, Editorial, for supervision of revisions and overall direction; Diane Goldschmidt, Managing Editor, for coordinating development of this edition; and Transcend Creative Services for typesetting this edition.

CHAPTER 1

Passing the CLEP Principles of Macroeconomics Exam

PASSING THE CLEP PRINCIPLES OF MACROECONOMICS EXAM

Congratulations! You're joining the millions of people who have discovered the value and educational advantage offered by the College Board's College-Level Examination Program, or CLEP. This test prep focuses on what you need to know to succeed on the CLEP Principles of Macroeconomics exam, and will help you earn the college credit you deserve while reducing your tuition costs.

GETTING STARTED

There are many different ways to prepare for a CLEP exam. What's best for you depends on how much time you have to study and how comfortable you are with the subject matter. To score your highest, you need a system that can be customized to fit you: your schedule, your learning style, and your current level of knowledge.

This book, and the online tools that come with it, allow you to create a personalized study plan through three simple steps: assessment of your knowledge, targeted review of exam content, and reinforcement in the areas where you need the most help.

Let's get started and see how this system works.

Test Yourself and Get Feedback	Assess your strengths and weaknesses. The score report from your online diagnostic exam gives you a fast way to pinpoint what you already know and where you need to spend more time studying.
Review with the Book	Armed with your diagnostic score report, review the parts of the book where you're weak and study the answer explanations for the test questions you answered incorrectly.
Ensure You're Ready for Test Day	After you've finished reviewing with the book, take our full-length practice tests. Review your score reports and re-study any topics you missed. We give you two full-length practice tests to ensure you're confident and ready for test day.

THE REA STUDY CENTER

The best way to personalize your study plan is to get feedback on what you know and what you don't know. At the online REA Study Center (*www.rea.com/studycenter*), you can access two types of assessment: a diagnostic exam and full-length practice exams. Each of these tools provides true-to-format questions and delivers a detailed score report that follows the topics set by the College Board.

Diagnostic Exam

Before you begin your review with the book, take the online diagnostic exam. Use your score report to help evaluate your overall understanding of the subject, so you can focus your study on the topics where you need the most review.

Full-Length Practice Exams

Our full-length practice tests give you the most complete picture of your strengths and weaknesses. After you've finished reviewing with the book, test what you've learned by taking the first of the two online practice exams. Review your score report, then go back and study any topics you missed. Take the second practice test to ensure you have mastered the material and are ready for test day.

If you're studying and don't have Internet access, you can take the printed tests in the book. These are the same practice tests offered at the REA Study Center, but without the added benefits of timed testing conditions and diagnostic score reports. Because the actual exam is Internet-based, we recommend you take at least one practice test online to simulate test-day conditions.

AN OVERVIEW OF THE EXAM

The CLEP Principles of Macroeconomics exam consists of approximately 80 multiple-choice questions, each with five possible answer choices, to be answered in 90 minutes.

The exam covers the material one would find in a college-level introductory macroeconomics course. The exam requires the test taker to understand concepts such as gross domestic product, consumption, and investment, and terms such as unemployment, inflation, inflationary gap and recessionary gap. Test takers should also understand the structure of the Federal Reserve Bank and the policies it uses to stabilize the economy. In addition, a basic understanding of foreign exchange markets, balance of payments, appreciation and depreciation of currencies is also expected.

The approximate breakdown of topics is as follows:

8-12%	Basic economic concepts
10-18%	Measurement of economic performance
60-70%	National income and price determination
10-15%	International economics and growth

CLEP and technology-enhanced questions

While most of the questions you will find on your CLEP exam will be standard multiple-choice questions, the College Board is now incorporating some technology-enhanced questions. These new question types include: filling in a numeric answer; shading areas of an object; or putting items in the correct order. In addition, several exams now have an optional essay section.

If you're familiar with basic computer skills, you'll have no trouble handling these question types if you encounter them on your exam.

ALL ABOUT THE CLEP PROGRAM

What is CLEP?

More adult learners use CLEP than any other credit-by-examination program in the United States. The CLEP program's 33 exams span five subject areas. The exams assess the material commonly required in an introductory-level college course. Based on recommendations from the American Council on Education, a passing score can earn you at least three credits per exam at more than 2,900 colleges and universities in the U.S. and abroad. Policies vary, so check with your school on the exams it accepts and the scores it requires. For a complete list of the CLEP subject examinations offered, visit the College Board website: *www.collegeboard.org/clep*.

Who takes CLEP exams?

CLEP exams are typically taken by people who have acquired knowledge outside the classroom and wish to bypass certain college courses and earn college credit. The CLEP program is designed to reward examinees for prior learning—no matter where or how that knowledge was acquired.

Although most CLEP examinees are adults returning to college, many home-schooled and high school students, traditional-age college students, military personnel, veterans, and international students take CLEP exams to earn college credit. There are no prerequisites, such as age or educational status, for taking CLEP examinations. However, because policies on granting credits vary among colleges, you should contact the particular institution from which you wish to receive CLEP credit.

How is my CLEP score determined?

Your CLEP score is based on two calculations. First, your CLEP raw score is figured; this is just the total number of test items you answer correctly. After the test is administered, your raw score is converted to a scaled score through a process called *equating*. Equating adjusts for minor variations in difficulty across test forms and among test items, and ensures that your score accurately represents your performance on the exam regardless of when or where you take it, or on how well others perform on the same test form.

Your scaled score is the number your college will use to determine if you've performed well enough to earn college credit. Scaled scores for the CLEP exams are delivered on a 20–80 scale. Institutions can set their own scores for granting college credit, but a good passing estimate (based on recommendations from the American Council on Education) is generally a scaled score of 50, which usually requires getting roughly 66% of the questions correct.

For more information on scoring, contact the institution where you wish to be awarded the credit.

Who administers the exam?

CLEP exams are developed by the College Board, administered by Educational Testing Service (ETS), and involve the assistance of educators from throughout the United States. The test development process is designed and implemented to ensure that the content and difficulty level of the test are appropriate.

When and where is the exam given?

CLEP exams are administered year-round at more than 1,800 test centers in the United States and abroad. To find the test center nearest you and to register for the exam, contact the CLEP Program:

CLEP Services
P.O. Box 6600
Princeton, NJ 08541-6600
Phone: (800) 257-9558 (8 A.M. to 6 P.M. ET)
Fax: (610) 628-3726
Website: *www.collegeboard.org/clep*

The CLEP iBT platform

To improve the testing experience for both institutions and test-takers, the College Board's CLEP Program has transitioned its 33 exams from the eCBT platform to an Internet-based testing (iBT) platform. All CLEP test-takers may now register for exams and manage their personal account information through the "My Account" feature on the CLEP website. This new feature simplifies the registration process and automatically downloads all pertinent information about the test session, making for a more streamlined check-in.

OPTIONS FOR MILITARY PERSONNEL AND VETERANS

CLEP exams are available free of charge to eligible military personnel as well as eligible civilian employees. All the CLEP exams are available at test centers on college campuses and military bases. Contact your Educational Services Officer or Navy College Education Specialist for more information. Visit the DANTES or College Board websites for details about CLEP opportunities for military personnel.

Eligible U.S. veterans can claim reimbursement for CLEP exams and administration fees pursuant to provisions of the Veterans Benefits Improvement Act of 2004. For details on eligibility and submitting a claim for reimbursement, visit the U.S. Department of Veterans Affairs website at *www.gibill.va.gov.*

CLEP can be used in conjunction with the Post-9/11 GI Bill, which applies to veterans returning from the Iraq and Afghanistan theaters of operation. Because the GI Bill provides tuition for up to 36 months, earning college credits with CLEP exams expedites academic progress and degree completion within the funded timeframe.

SSD ACCOMMODATIONS FOR CANDIDATES WITH DISABILITIES

Many test candidates qualify for extra time to take the CLEP exams, but you must make these arrangements in advance. For information, contact:

College Board Services for Students with Disabilities
P.O. Box 8060
Mt. Vernon, Illinois 62864-0060
Phone: (609) 771-7137 (Monday through Friday, 8 A.M. to 6 P.M. ET)
TTY: (609) 882-4118
Fax: (866) 360-0114
E-mail: ssd@info.collegeboard.org

6-WEEK STUDY PLAN

Although our study plan is designed to be used in the six weeks before your exam, it can be condensed to three weeks by combining each two-week period into one.

Be sure to set aside enough time—at least two hours each day—to study. The more time you spend studying, the more prepared and relaxed you will feel on the day of the exam.

Week	Activity
1	Take the Diagnostic Exam at the online REA Study Center. The score report will identify topics where you need the most review.
2–4	Study the review focusing on the topics you missed (or were unsure of) on the Diagnostic Exam.
5	Take Practice Test 1 at the REA Study Center. Review your score report and re-study any topics you missed.
6	Take Practice Test 2 at the REA Study Center to see how much your score has improved. If you still got a few questions wrong, go back to the review and study any topics you may have missed.

TEST-TAKING TIPS

Know the format of the test. Familiarize yourself with the CLEP computer screen beforehand by logging on to the College Board website. Waiting until test day to see what it looks like in the pretest tutorial risks injecting needless anxiety into your testing experience. Also, familiarizing yourself with the directions and format of the exam will save you valuable time on the day of the actual test.

Read all the questions—completely. Make sure you understand each question before looking for the right answer. Reread the question if it doesn't make sense.

Read all of the answers to a question. Just because you think you found the correct response right away, do not assume that it's the best answer. The last answer choice might be the correct answer.

Work quickly and steadily. You will have 90 minutes to answer approximately 80 questions, so work quickly and steadily. Taking the timed practice tests online will help you learn how to budget your time.

Use the process of elimination. Stumped by a question? Don't make a random guess. Eliminate as many of the answer choices as possible. By eliminating just two answer choices, you give yourself a better chance of getting the item correct, since there will only be three choices left from which to make your guess. Remember, your score is based only on the number of questions you answer correctly.

Don't waste time! Don't spend too much time on any one question. Your time is limited, so pacing yourself is very important. Work on the easier questions first. Skip the difficult questions and go back to them if you have the time.

Look for clues to answers in other questions. If you skip a question you don't know the answer to, you might find a clue to the answer elsewhere on the test.

Be sure that your answer registers before you go to the next item. Look at the screen to see that your mouse-click causes the pointer to darken the proper oval. If your answer doesn't register, you won't get credit for that question.

THE DAY OF THE EXAM

On test day, you should wake up early (after a good night's rest, of course) and have breakfast. Dress comfortably, so you are not distracted by being too hot or too cold while taking the test. (Note that "hoodies" are not allowed.) Arrive at the test center early. This will allow you to collect your thoughts and relax before the test, and it will also spare you the anxiety that comes with being late. As an added incentive, keep in mind that no one will be allowed into the test session after the test has begun.

Before you leave for the test center, make sure you have your admission form and another form of identification, which must contain a recent photograph, your name, and signature (i.e., driver's license, student identification card, or current alien registration card). You will not be admitted to the test center if you do not have proper identification.

You may not wear a digital watch (wrist or pocket), alarm watch, or wrist-watch camera. In addition, no cell phones, dictionaries, textbooks, notebooks, briefcases, or packages will be permitted, and drinking, smoking, and eating are prohibited.

Good luck on the CLEP Principles of Macroeconomics exam!

CHAPTER 2

Basic Economic Concepts Review

BASIC ECONOMIC CONCEPTS REVIEW

KEY TERMS

- Scarcity
- Needs and Wants
- Origin of Economics
- Economic Choice
- Trade-offs
- PPF Curve
- Law of Diminishing Marginal Returns
- Law of Increasing Opportunity Cost
- Laws of Supply and Demand
- Determinants of Supply
- Law of Diminishing Marginal Utility
- Determinants of Demand
- Change in Quantity Supplied or Demanded
- Change in Supply or Demand
- Markets
- Equilibrium Price
- Shortage
- Surplus
- Productive Efficiency
- Allocative Efficiency
- Market Equilibrium
- Consumer Surplus
- Producer Surplus

- Four Factors of Production (Inputs)
- Types of Economic Systems
- Circular Flow Model

ECONOMIC FOUNDATIONS

The study of economics involves a specific way of looking at how things work in the world. This approach has three main components: economic methods, macroeconomics, and microeconomics. Adam Smith is considered the "founding father" of economics, and his book *The Wealth of Nations* presented many of the concepts upon which this course is based. Since his work was published (in 1776), many others have furthered the study of economics, though they certainly have not always agreed with Smith. In fact, four general—and differing—viewpoints have evolved regarding the workings of markets: Classical, Keynesian, Monetary, and Neo-classical. These differing schools of thought will be discussed in the Macroeconomics review.

SCARCITY AND ECONOMIC CHOICE

Economics is always about limits. We are, by the very nature of our existence, limited to the resources provided by the planet. Our wants and needs, however, are not limited, and therein lies the rub! The result is scarcity, the fundamental reality of economics. Because of scarcity, humankind must engage in production choices. The primary decision asks: Which of our needs and wants do we satisfy, and which go unfulfilled? Answering this question forces people to make choices, and trade-offs result. Economists help us to understand these choices and the variety of possibilities that we face. Economists employ models that help us to focus on specific relationships that exist in the production and consumption of goods and services. These models employ the scientific method, in that they apply logical analysis based on economic principles to predict and explain outcomes, as well as suggest policies.

TRADE-OFFS AND OPPORTUNITY COST

Another basic observation of economics is that the economic choices we make result in trade-offs that can be measured. As those trade-offs are measured, we realize that various combinations of goods and services can be produced. However, as we produce more of one good, we incur a cost, in the form of lost production of an alternative good or service. The PPF Curve, the Law of Diminishing Marginal Returns, and the Law of Increasing Opportunity Cost help us to understand this axiom. Together, these realities govern the behavior of the supplier in the free market system. Let's start our review with a look at the PPF Curve.

Figure 2-1 Production Possibilities Frontier Curve

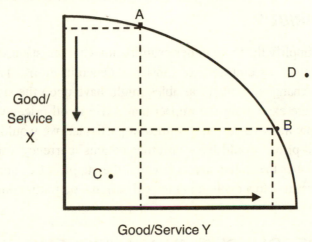

Good/Service Y

Figure 2-1 shows that as you move from point A to point B along the production curve, the quantity of Y produced increases, but the quantity of X decreases. In other words, you sacrifice X to gain Y. This is termed *opportunity cost*. The curve is bowed outward to represent the economic reality that as an input of production is used up, its output diminishes. The reverse of this procedure, a sacrifice of Y in order to produce more X, is possible as well. The curve represents the maximum possible combinations available. It is possible for an economy to produce inside the curve at C, a point that represents underusage of production inputs. The point of production represented by D is not possible given the current inputs (resources) present in the economy; to achieve D would require economic growth resulting from an increase in the inputs of production.

THEORETICAL ECONOMICS

Economists develop models of behavior focused on the forces that produce goods and services and those who consume them. Due to the complexity of the innumerable variable forces at work in the real world, economists attempt to reduce the study at hand to those facts that they deem most relevant. In doing so they attempt to develop hypotheses (such as cause-and-effect relationships) that lead them to generalize and develop principles or laws that predict probable outcomes of economic actions. Several key elements are necessary to assist in the formation of economic models and laws.

ECONOMIC METHODOLOGY

CETERIS PARIBUS

In order to simplify the topic under examination economist's use the "all other things being equal" assumption to construct generalizations. This eliminates the impact that changes in other variables might have upon the study topic. For example, if we are examining the impact that a rise in oil prices would have on the U.S. economy and our currency values in particular, we would eliminate the impact those oil prices would have on other nations' currency values. Thus we could conclude that the dollar appreciates as the supply of dollars in currency markets decreases due to a decline in our real national output/income.

FALLACY OF COMPOSITION AND "POST HOC" FALLACY

Two other pitfalls that economists must be wary of are the fallacy of composition and the "Post Hoc" fallacy as they interfere with sound reasoning. The fallacy of composition simply means that one must not assume that what applies in one instance is true for the whole. For example, if you go to a comedy club and you find the first comic to be hilarious, it would be faulty to assume that all of the comics that night will be equally so! The Post Hoc fallacy simply supposes that if one event follows another the former is the cause of the latter. For example, to conclude that the sun rises due to the crowing of a rooster would certainly heighten the importance of roosters to our survival.

MARGINAL ANALYSIS

Finally, a major analytical tool employed by economists is marginal analysis. Simply put, marginal analysis entails the impact of one more or one less variable upon an economic outcome. For example, if a firm hired one more worker, how much would the output of the firm increase or decrease? The use of marginality helps economists predict decision making in the economy as one can determine a marginal benefit or a marginal cost relationship. With this in mind it is easy to understand the use of graphs by economists in their study of economic relationships. A graph allows economists to quantify and record the relationship between two variables on the X (independent variable) and Y (dependent variable) axis. The positive or negative slope that results from the plotting of data reveals a general direct (positive, upward slope) or indirect (negative, downward slope) relationship. The calculation of the slope of the linear relationship of the variables is also very significant in predicting the infinite outcome of various combinations of two items.

ORIGINS OF SUPPLY

Figure 2-2   Law of Diminishing Marginal Returns

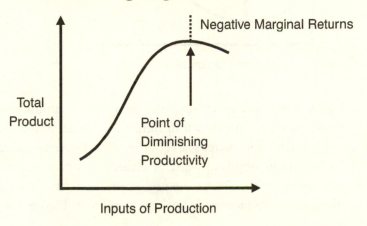

The model in figure 2-2 shows the relationship between the inputs of production and the total production resulting from those inputs. The inputs of production are: raw material, labor, capital (money or goods), and entrepreneurship. Initially, as we increase the factors of production, output increases at an increasing rate. At some point, however, additional inputs not only create output at a diminishing rate, but actually decrease the total output. The production table (table 2-1) demonstrates that relationship. Notice that as the third input is added to production, the total output increases from 12 to 16, but the marginal rate of change has decreased from 7 units gained to only 4 units of gained production. This is a diminishing rate, hence the name *Law of Diminishing Marginal Returns*. When the fifth input is added, the total productivity actually decreases from 16 to 12, a loss of 4 units.

Table 2-1

Input	1	2	3	4	5
Output	5	12	16	16	12

Figure 2-3   Law of Increasing Opportunity Costs

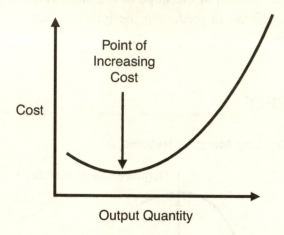

There is a clear relationship between the decrease in productivity and the increase in opportunity cost. As shown in figure 2-3, when productivity diminishes, the cost of production increases. This is what governs the law of supply and is why the graph slopes upward. A change in price causes movement along the supply curve. Why? Because a higher price covers the higher cost of increased production; more product is brought to market. Figure 2-4 shows this direct relationship.

DETERMINANTS OF SUPPLY

Determinants of supply (that is, the prices of raw materials, labor, capital, and entrepreneurship) may cause the curve to shift (see figure 2-5). An increase in the price of the inputs of production causes a contraction in supply. This is shown as an upward and leftward movement of the supply curve. If input prices decrease, the supply curve moves downward and to the right, representing an overall increase in supply. Because the producer's cost of production begins to increase at some point, a producer must receive a higher sales price to be induced to make additional product. Remember, a producer is driven by profit, and maximum profit is the goal. Therefore, producers seek minimum cost per unit of production for the highest productive efficiency.

Figure 2-4   Law of Supply

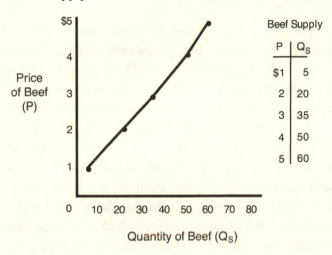

If the determinants of supply reduce the cost of production, the supply curve shifts from S_1 to S_2 (as shown in figure 2-5). This shift represents an overall increase in the quantity of goods brought to market at lower prices. If the determinants of supply increase the cost of production, the supply curve shifts from S_3 to S_1. This change in supply represents a decrease in the quantity of goods brought to market at higher prices.

Figure 2-5   Shifts of Supply

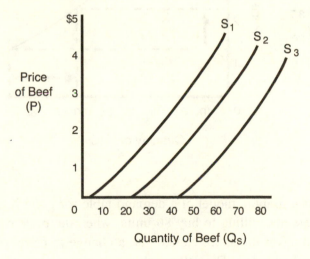

ORIGINS OF DEMAND

Increasing opportunity costs cause producers to behave in a predictable manner. Consumers also behave in a predictable manner because of scarcity. Consumers seek goods and services to satisfy their needs and wants. Though our needs and wants are unlimited, both the existence and the availability of the economic resources necessary to meet those needs are limited. Economic systems are developed to address this basic conflict. In a free market system, our income limits our ability to satisfy our desires (this is called the *rationing power* of prices). Economists believe that consumer satisfaction can be measured, since consumers attach a dollar value to goods and services (g/s). The more satisfaction derived from a g/s, the higher the price you are willing to pay. When we measure a group of consumers, we determine their demand schedule for a particular item. Price serves as a means of rationing the g/s produced.

Figure 2-6   Demand

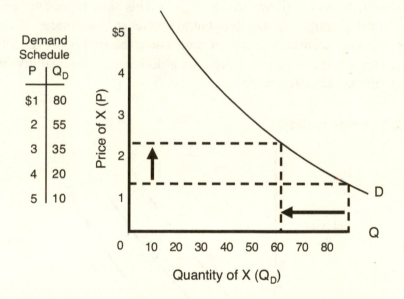

Figure 2-6 is a graphic model of a demand table for good X. At a low price of $1, consumers are willing to buy 80 units; when the price rises to $2, consumers demand fewer units, 55. Notice that a change in price causes a change in the quantity demanded. The relationship between a change in price and a change in quantity demanded is a basic economic understanding. A primary feature of demand is that as price rises, the quantity demanded falls; and as

price falls, the quantity demanded increases. Economists call this inverse relationship the *Law of Demand*. Why is this inverse relationship always present in
consumer behavior? The primary answer stems from the nature of humankind,
established in the law of diminishing marginal utility.

Figure 2-7 Diminishing Marginal Utility

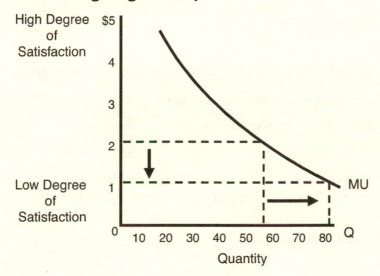

Economists can survey a group of consumers to measure the relationship
between their satisfaction with a particular item (expressed in terms of the
money they are willing to give up in exchange for that item) and the quantity
of that item they possess. Figure 2-7 shows that as the quantity increases, satisfaction declines. For example, as the quantity increases from 55 units to 80
units, satisfaction diminishes from 2 to 1. This is an inverse relationship. Notice
also that as the quantity of the good increases, the consumer values the product
less; a change in price causes movement along the utility curve. As a consumer
increases consumption of a good or service, the marginal utility obtained from
each additional unit decreases. This principle, called the *Law of Diminishing
Marginal Utility*, is what governs consumer behavior. The more of something I
have, the less I value it. Consumers tell producers by their dollar expenditures
the quantity of output they are willing to buy at various prices. To entice consumers to purchase increased quantity, producers must lower the price. This
principle is the guiding hand behind the law of demand.

DETERMINANTS OF DEMAND

Because consumer (sovereignty) demand may change at any time (figure 2-8), the entire schedule may shift outward (D_2 to D_3) signaling greater demand; or inward (D_2 to D_1), indicating less demand. These changes in demand are caused by a group of factors called the *determinants of demand*:

- Tastes and preferences

- Income

- Price and availability of substitute and complementary goods

- Future price or quantity expectations

- Number of buyers (population size)

- Government regulation

So, for example, if red shirts became trendy, the demand for red shirts would shift outward, resulting in higher prices and greater quantity bought.

Figure 2-8   Shifts in Demand

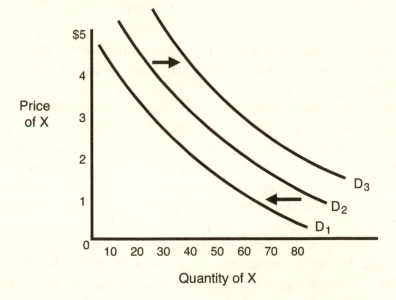

MARKETS

DETERMINING PRICE AND QUANTITY

The forces of supply and demand come together in the marketplace. The market is a mechanism, a place where buyers and sellers of goods and services meet to satisfy their self-interest. The invisible forces of supply and demand interact to determine the price and quantity of goods bought and sold in the marketplace. The model portrayed in figure 2-9 assumes that competition is present for both producers and consumers. Free markets seek a balance between the interests of buyer and seller. This compromise point is known as the *equilibrium price*. It is the point at which supply and demand intersect. Equilibrium is significant, for it is at this price and quantity that the market clears, the price stabilizes, and product is available. Move from this price or quantity, and either shortage (inadequate supply of goods) or surplus (excess unsold goods) results. Economists have developed a graphic model of this event.

Figure 2-9 Market Equilibrium

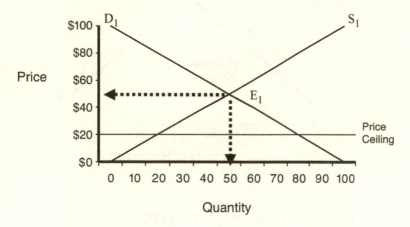

CONSUMER, PRODUCER SURPLUS AND MARKET EFFICIENCY

What makes markets so efficient in the organization of economic activity is the role of consumer and producer surplus. Consumer surplus as depicted in figure 2-10 refers to the portion of the demand curve that lies above the equilibrium point. This portion of the demand curve represents those consumers that value the good so highly they would be willing to pay a higher price to attain it. Any rise in price would reduce consumer surplus and a fall would increase it.

Producer surplus refers to those suppliers that would be willing to bring their goods to market at an even lower price. Any rise in price would increase producer surplus and a fall would decrease it. When added together we realize the total surplus that represents the total benefit to society from the production and consumption of the good. Notice that maximum total surplus is present at equilibrium.

Figure 2-10   Consumer and Producer Surplus

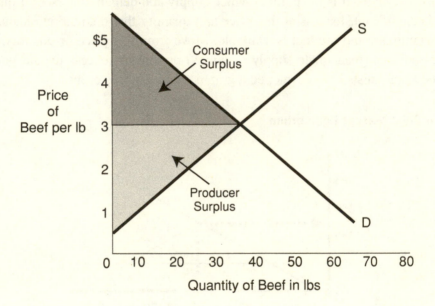

REALLOCATION REDUCES SURPLUS

As pictured in Figure 2-11, Consumer A is willing to pay $4.00 a lb for beef while Consumer D is only willing to pay $2.00. Now suppose that we take beef from A and give it to D, consumer surplus would decline from $4.00 to $2.00. Simply put, A has had a highly valued good taken away and given to another that values it less. Thus, total surplus of satisfaction declines by $2.00 and the total benefit to society would decline as well.

Now view figure 2-11 from the producer standpoint. Assume that Producer B has a cost of $4.00 per lb while Producer C has a cost of $2.00 per lb. At an equilibrium price of $3.00 per lb, Producer C would provide the market with beef (the cost of production is less than sales price = profit/happy) and Producer B would not (the cost of production is higher than the sales price = loss/unhappy). However, if we forced Producer B to provide goods and reduced sales by Producer C, producer surplus would decline by $2.00 as would total surplus and the total benefit would fall by $2.00 as well.

Later in this review we will return to this concept as it is the basis for analysis of the effect of government intervention into markets through introduction of tax, subsidy, price ceiling and floor.

Figure 2-11   Consumer and Producer Surplus

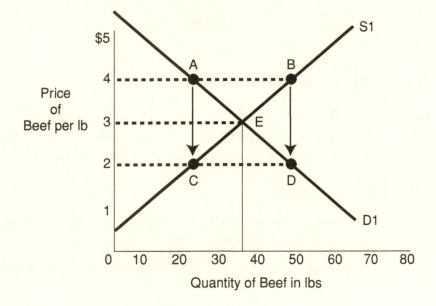

MARKET REACTION TO CHANGE IN CONSUMER AND PRODUCER SURPLUS

If the determinants of supply or demand cause a change in either demand or supply, both price equilibrium and quantity change. For example, let's say that figure 2-12 shows the model for the canned tuna market operating at E_1. If there were a fish disease outbreak and tuna became less available, the supply curve would shift inward, to the left, resulting in a higher equilibrium price of tuna and lower equilibrium quantity at E_2.

Figure 2-12 Tuna Market Equilibrium

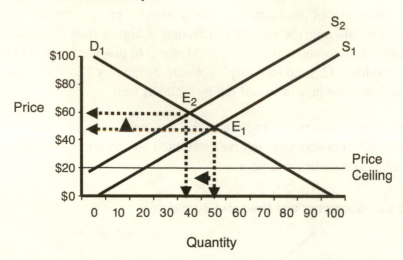

FOUR RESOURCE INPUTS

In markets, the forces of supply and demand are constantly at work. Economic systems organize society's decisions regarding the use of resources. Production of all goods and services requires four main resource inputs:

1. Land—raw materials.

2. Capital—means of production (investment goods) and finance capital (money used to acquire capital goods).

3. Labor—human resources, including both manual and intellectual skills.

4. Entrepreneurship—business organization and/or innovation.

FOUR MAIN ECONOMIC SYSTEMS

Over the years, humankind has organized the means and distribution of production into four economic system types. Those systems are:

1. Free market—consumers and producers operate in an unregulated environment.

2. Traditional—society does not change its methods of production or consumption.

3. Command (state centrally planned)—government agencies regulate production and consumption.

4. Mixed market—system blends free market, traditional, and state planning. (In recent years the mixed market system has become increasingly prevalent as the command economies have failed (USSR) or modified (China) by adapting more free market features.)

All of these systems hold in common the need to answer the same three basic questions:

1. Which goods and services to produce?

2. How to produce goods and services?

3. To whom to distribute the goods and services?

CIRCULAR FLOW MODEL

Today, nearly all of the world's nations employ some form of the market system. It is critical that we understand the key decision makers and main markets present in this system, which is governed by supply and demand. The circular flow model (figure 2-13) helps us to see the two main decision makers in a free market: Households and Businesses.

CONSUMER AND PRODUCER

The two main markets where these two groups interact are the *resource* (input factor) *market* and the *product market*. Input resources flow from the Household to Businesses in the resource market. This purchase of input from the Household is the cost of production to a business. The sale of these resources by Households to Businesses generates Household income (wages, rents, interest, and profits). Remember, one of the key features of a free market economy is that the means (inputs) of production are owned by the individual. The product market is the place where Businesses sell their goods and services to Households. This sale to the Household is the source of a Business's revenue. When a Business subtracts its costs from this revenue, profit/loss is determined. This consumption of goods and services by Households is where the income earned from the resource market is expended. When a Household subtracts its consumption expenditures from its income, savings or debt are determined.

Figure 2-13   Circular Flow Model

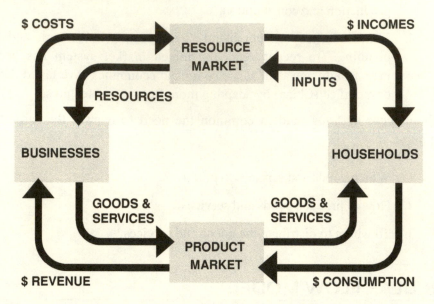

Now add the public sector of Government to the private sector of Households and Businesses (figure 2-14) on the circular flow model. Notice that the Government purchases goods and services from the product market and employs input factors from the resource market. These purchases are the origin of our public goods, such as roads and bridges. Government finances its purchases through taxation of the private sector. This flow of goods, services, and tax dollars (subsidy and transfer payments) suggests how Government might try, through fiscal policy, to stabilize the economy.

Figure 2-14   Circular Flow Model

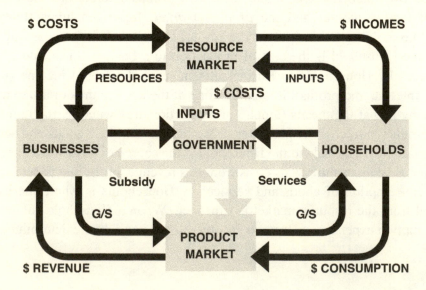

Today, the majority of the world's nations have agreed to follow many of these principles, and joined together in the World Trade Organization. This organization has contributed to increased specialization in the world, creating greater productive efficiency. Nations today seek absolute or comparative advantage in production, resulting in greater trade and thus increasing their standard of living. This freer international trade has greatly increased global competition, which affects a large number of U.S. firms. The supporters and critics of free trade continue to debate the advantages and disadvantages of this mixed market system. Nonetheless, imports and exports play a role in our economy. Imports and exports are the final link in the chain that forms our economy (figure 2-15). To see this, we return to the circular flow model for a last time.

Figure 2-15   Circular Flow Model

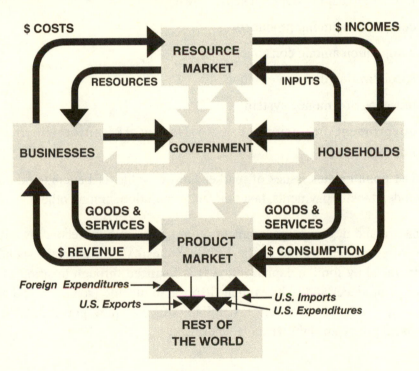

Notice in figure 2-15 that when the United States exports goods and services to the rest of the world, wealth from those other nations flows into ours. The opposite is also true: when we purchase foreign goods and services (import), our wealth flows into the foreign producer. This forms the basis for the balance of trade (examined in greater detail later). Essentially, exports add to our wealth (favorable balance of trade) while imports subtract from our wealth (unfavorable balance of trade). Also note that imports increase goods and services available for domestic consumption.

FREE MARKET ECONOMY PRINCIPLES

The United States has a mixed market economy, primarily employing free market principles. Among the most important characteristics of a market system are:

- private property
- freedom to enter or exit production markets
- freedom to dispose of your property as you see fit
- freedom to work in any area for which you are qualified
- freedom to buy goods and services that satisfy your wants
- freedom to act in your own self-interest
- competition among producers
- competition among consumers
- specialization/division of labor
- presence of a money system
- government provision of legal framework, enforcement, and infra-structure

This last point creates issues of market failure, spillover benefits and costs, public goods, transfer payments, taxation, and regulation, among others.

The nature and degree of government intervention into our economy causes constant, often heated, debate in the United States. All government spending (unless financed by foreign capital inflows) is financed through taxation of the consumer or producer and reduces their disposable income (seen as a leakage). This flow of goods, services and tax dollars suggests how government tries, through fiscal policy, to stabilize the economy.

CHAPTER 3

CLEP Macroeconomics Course Review

MACROECONOMICS REVIEW

KEY TERMS

- GDP
- Aggregate expenditure
- AE model
- Inflation
- Inflation expectations
- Stagflation
- CPI
- PCE
- Real GDP
- Nominal GDP
- GDP deflator
- Cost-push inflation
- Demand-pull inflation
- Keynesian theory
- Say's Law
- Supply side
- Demand side
- Laffer curve
- Short-run Phillips Curve
- Long-run Phillips Curve
- Marginal propensity to consume
- Marginal propensity to save
- Equilibrium GDP

- GDP multiplier
- Investment demand
- AD/AS model
- Monetary policy
- Fiscal policy
- Cyclical deficits
- National Debt
- Crowding out
- Money supply
- Stocks
- Bonds
- Federal Reserve System
- Banks
- Loanable funds
- Real interest rates
- Nominal interest rates
- Money multiplier
- Balance sheet
- FOMC
- Expansionary policy
- Contractionary policy
- Policy mix
- NAFTA
- GATT
- WTO
- Global economy
- Comparative advantage
- Absolute advantage
- Balance of payments
- Current account
- Capital account
- Capital inflows
- Fixed or floating exchange rates

Macroeconomics is the study of the overall performance of an economy. Critical to an understanding of macroeconomics is the role of economic indicators. Hundreds of different indicators are available today, all measuring different aspects of our complicated system. We will focus on the key indicators that paint a picture of an economy in broad strokes. These indicators fall into three main categories: leading, coincidental, and lagging. Based on our earlier investigation of the circular flow model, it is easy to understand that the first logical indicator of the state of our economic performance is a measure of the dollar flow of payments for input resources or the output value of goods and services consumed. Each is measured by a different government agency: output by the Department of Commerce, and income by the Internal Revenue Service.

MEASURING ECONOMIC PERFORMANCE

The basic measurement used by economists to gauge the overall state of the economy today is gross domestic product (GDP), defined as the dollar value of all final goods and services produced within the nation's borders within one year. The ownership of the firm is not an issue, only the domestic origin of the good or service. This also explains why the original GNP (gross national product) indicator has been replaced by GDP, as GNP measures g/s produced by U.S. businesses regardless of location. So, a good produced by a British-owned company in the United States would have its production value (excluding profits taken back to Britain) added to GDP but not GNP. By the same token, a good produced in Mexico City by a U.S. company would not be included in GDP (except profits brought back to the United States), but would be counted in GNP. Thus, GDP is the sum of all the money spent purchasing final goods and services produced in the United States, regardless of firm ownership.

Another way to measure economic activity is to measure the income derived or earned by creating those goods and services. Therefore, we can measure productivity by a national income approach or a national expenditure approach; in the end, they should be equal. This is a lagging indicator, in that it measures an event that has already happened.

The expenditure measurement consists of four components: household consumption expenditure (C), gross business domestic investment (Ig), government purchases (G), and net foreign purchases (Xn) (subtract import value, as foreign goods are not a part of U.S. productivity). This can be stated as a simple formula:

$$C + Ig + G + Xn$$

The national income measurement totals five main sources of income: wages, salaries, rents, interest, and profits from business ownership (including sole proprietorships, partnerships, and private and public corporations).

One of the key issues in the creation of this indicator is possible change in money value over time; that is, inflation or deflation. Economists deal with this issue by distinguishing between nominal measurement (current dollars) and real measurement (reflecting changes in price levels or constant dollars). If one wants to use GDP in a comparative manner—say, GDP in 1999 compared to the GDP in 2000—real GDP must be used, or any conclusion reached would be flawed.

ECONOMIC PERFORMANCE OVER TIME

Economic growth is an increase in real GDP. Economic contraction is a decrease in real GDP. Total expenditure is the immediate determinant of output, and thus of unemployment/employment and inflation/deflation. The business cycle, depicted in figure 3-1, is a way of explaining change in aggregate expenditure.

There are five parts to the business cycle:

- Expansion
- Peak
- Contraction (recession)
- Trough (bottom)
- Recovery

Figure 3-1   Business Cycle

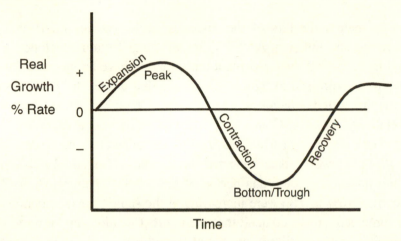

The time and degree of each phase varies. The generally accepted definition of a recession is six months of negative GDP growth. Many things can cause fluctuations in economic expenditure. Some cycle changes result from seasonal change; others are due to technological innovation, political events such as war, money supply and interest rates, or even the degree of household debt. Regardless of the cause, a change in total spending results in a change in total output. Economists try to track and predict these movements by economic indicators. These indicators fall into three categories:

- Leading (predict a change)
- Coincidental (happen at the same time)
- Lagging (after the change)

All three types of indicators are useful. During recession or expansion, g/s experience different rates of change. Goods seem to experience a greater degree of change than services. Durable (lasting longer than three years) and capital goods show a greater degree of change than nondurable goods (lifespan less than three years). Nondurable goods tend to be less expensive and necessary. Durable goods tend to be expensive, somewhat of a luxury, and their purchase is thus more postponable.

PHILLIPS CURVE

The two main indicators of the business cycle, besides GDP change, are unemployment and inflation. A.W. Phillips of Great Britain developed a theory, published in 1958, that unemployment and inflation have an inverse relationship. The concept is expressed in figure 3-2. Notice that during the 1960s, when this theory was first tested, inflation was at a relatively high 7%, while unemployment was a relatively low 4%. Conversely, when inflation was a relatively low 3%, unemployment was a high 6%. This theory was apparently confirmed throughout the 1960s. However, data collected during the 1970s and 1980s called the theory into question. During this period of time, both inflation (3% to 7%) and unemployment (6% to 7%) were increasing at the same time (stagflation). In retrospect, some economists contend that the indirect relationship between inflation and unemployment was still present but at overall higher levels. The cause of this behavior was cost-push inflation due to the rising price of oil during the energy crises in 1974 and 1980. Also, the very low levels of both inflation and unemployment during the 1990s were most likely due to the increased productivity experienced during this decade. This topic is revisited during discussion of the AD/AS model, as well as the debate over best practices for management of an economy.

Figure 3-2   Phillips Curve

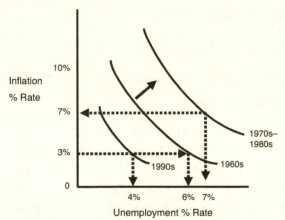

The question remains: Is there an inverse relationship (trade off) between inflation and unemployment? The neoclassical point of view believes no, not in the long run. They believe there is always a movement to a macroeconomic equilibrium at full employment (maximum potential output). This is arrived at as the utility maximizing components of the economy (supply of and demand for labor) arrive at the market clearing price of labor through price and wage adjustments (figure 3-3).

Figure 3-3   Phillips Curve (Long-Run) LRAS = NRU (full employment)

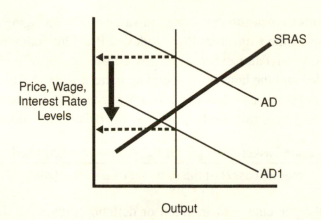

Determining unemployment is relatively simple (*labor force* is defined as the number able and willing to work):

$$\text{unemployment rate} = \frac{\text{unemployed}}{\text{labor force}} \times 100$$

However, using unemployment as an indicator of the state of the economy requires adjustment. There are three types of unemployment:

- structural (mismatch of skills or job location)
- frictional (between jobs)
- cyclical (due to decline in total spending)

Cyclical unemployment gives economists the best picture of the state of the economy. Therefore, to determine cyclical unemployment, the natural rate of unemployment (structural and frictional, which varies over time) must be subtracted from total unemployment. So, full employment in economic terms does not mean 100% employment. If cyclical unemployment were at 0%, we would realize our full production possibility. Government guarantee of full employment is a hotly debated political issue.

CONSUMER PRICE INDEX

Another means to measure the change in value due to changing prices, inflation, or deflation is the Consumer Price Index (CPI). This index is determined much like the GDP deflator except that only consumer out-of-pocket expenditures are included and the household spending pattern is fixed. This answers the question, how much more or less did consumers spend on the same goods this year compared to a fixed time in the past? The formula for the index is:

$$CPI = \frac{\text{market basket of set g/s for the year to be determined}}{\text{market basket of the same set of g/s for a base}} \times 100$$

This gives the percentage of inflation or deflation present in that year on a constant set of goods. This is a lagging indicator, as it measures an event that has already happened. For example:

1982–1984	100.0 base year
1999	166.6
2000	172.2

The inflation rate for 2000 was 3.4%; (172.2 − 166.6) ÷ 166.6 = 3.4%.

Shortcomings of this approach include:

- changing spending patterns (consumers shift purchases in response to changes in relative prices)

- new products (either not included in basket or weighted improperly)

- quality improvements (leading to greater reliability)

The reality is that the market basket of g/s we purchase changes over time, and the percentage of income spent on a specific g/s may also change. This would result in over- or understating the rate of inflation/deflation. This may prove especially troubling when the CPI is employed by government to adjust transfer payments such as Social Security.

GDP PRICE INDEX

The deflator formula is: Real GDP = Nominal GDP/Price Index (see CPI).

A price index is determined by measuring the price of a basket of g/s in a base year and dividing it by the price of the same basket of goods in the year to be determined, times 100. This percentage of change yields the price index in nominal GDP relative to the index year. Another method is to divide nominal GDP by real GDP, which gives a GDP price index. This analysis answers the question: How much more did it cost to buy what I bought today compared to yesterday? This index is a broader measure of inflation than the CPI because it includes not just the consumer, but government, industry, and foreign consumption. Again, the flaw here is that it assumes that people do not substitute goods as prices change. We know that in a short period of time (one quarter to the next) this would result in a fairly accurate price comparison, however, it is simply not true over a longer period of time because people do substitute goods as prices change. For example:

Year	Nominal GDP	Real GDP	GDP Price Index
1970	5680.0	6548.0	86.7
1980	7407.2	7407.2	100.0
1990	9864.5	8432.6	116.98

This table establishes 1980 as the base index year and recognizes that nominal GDP in 1970 was undervalued, as the dollar was worth more in 1970 than in 1980 or 1990. Thus, 1970 GDP was understated. Conversely, this index would show that nominal GDP in 1990 was overstated, due to inflation that had occurred since the base year. Unlike the fixed-weight CPI, the GDP deflator tends to systematically understate inflation as substitution is not a factor.

PERSONAL CONSUMPTION EXPENDITURE INDEX

The aforementioned shortcomings of the CPI and the deflator have caused some economists (especially at the Federal Reserve) to turn to a third measurement tool of inflation. This indicator is the Personal Consumption Expenditure (PCE) "chain type" index. A chain type index is midway between a fixed weight and a deflator. The PCE asks the question: How much would it cost people to buy the same goods and services that they actually bought last year? By making a price change link from one year to the next, the overstatement of the CPI and the understatement of inflation by the GDP deflator are greatly reduced. Another major difference is that, unlike the CPI, the PCE includes medical expenditures, which is mainly funded by employer-funded insurance, or government programs such as Medicaid and Medicare. Medical costs have been increasing at a very rapid rate so, if not included, one could see that inflation would be vastly understated.

WHY DOES THE INFLATION INDICATOR TYPE MATTER?

All three indicators draw upon the same data of final retail sales price, yet differ in how the data is weighted, and what is included. The differences are dramatic, especially in the medical area. In the CPI, medical costs make up only about 4% of the total market basket, yet, in the PCE it accounts for close to 15%, a statistically significant weight. Another area of significant deviation is housing. In the CPI, housing is about 40% of the index, whereas in the PCE, it's closer to 20%, again significant in determining inflation outcomes.

The type of indicator used matters most in the creation of monetary policy (covered in greater detail later). In the U.S., the Federal Reserve (through the FOMC) is charged with maintaining a rather vague "price stability," while in some European countries they actually have a published targeted inflation rate. Since the degree of inflation present in the economy varies based upon the indicator used, it matters in determining short-run policy, however, in the long run they do tend to move in conjunction. In reality, a good economist uses all three indicators and is very concerned with identifying the source of deviation between them.

EFFECTS OF INFLATION

Inflation harms some, helps others, and leaves still others unaffected. Fixed-income recipients (retirees on private pensions or fixed annuities) are harmed by inflation because their spending/income power diminishes. Savers (retirement plans with fixed assets such as bonds) see the relative spending power of their money diminish, and creditors (banks) that have lent money at a fixed rate of return receive repayment in less valuable dollars. Debtors benefit from unanticipated inflation as they pay back loans with cheaper dollars. Individuals or firms that enjoy pricing power may see revenue grow faster than costs rise (real estate values). The effects of deflation are, of course, the opposite of these inflation scenarios.

TYPES OF INFLATION

There are two different types of inflation: cost-push and demand-pull. Cost-push inflation is generally due to an unexpected rise in resource inputs, sometimes termed a "supply shock" by economists. As prices rise in reaction, and quantity demanded decreases, firms produce fewer g/s and lay off workers. Two examples of this type of inflation occurred in 1972–1975 and in 1979–1980. In both instances the rapid increase in energy costs, triggered by OPEC oil price increases, led to reduction in output, higher prices, and increased unemployment. Some economists call this stagflation. Resource cost-push inflation is graphed in figure 3-4.

Figure 3-4   Cost-Push Inflation

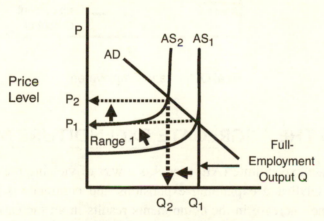

Real Output and Employment

Economists differ on the harm or benefits of mild inflation (less than 3%). Those who claim that any inflation is harmful point to the costs to businesses and households associated with price changes. In contrast, some believe that minor inflation provides a cushion of money necessary to maintaining strong levels of spending, full employment, high profits, and expansion of productivity.

Demand-pull inflation occurs when price levels rise rapidly because of total spending in excess of total productivity. This excess demand quickly bids up the price of available goods. This is often described as too much money pursuing too few goods.

In extreme cases of hyperinflation, as seen in figure 3-5, panic over increasingly worthless money may throw an economy into a state of barter and unemployment in which economic, social, and political upheaval occurs.

Therefore, prevention of hyperinflation is one of the most significant missions of government. However, determining the causes of inflation is difficult, as is finding a cure.

Figure 3-5 Demand-Pull Inflation

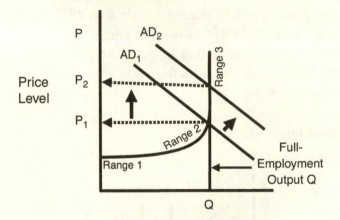

Real Output and Employment

BUILDING THE AGGREGATE EXPENDITURE MODEL

The aggregate expenditure (AE) model is a way of viewing the components that make up GDP and explaining expansions and contractions in the business cycle. A net increase in the components results in an increase in GDP. A net decrease in a component results in a decrease in GDP. This way of viewing GDP is sometimes referred to as *leakage and injection analysis*. Knowledge of this concept allows one to attempt to influence growth or contraction in the business cycle. The agent responsible for this management, as well as the nature and degree of intervention, leads to an ongoing and, often heated, economic debate.

THE GREAT DEBATE

The AE model attacks the foundation of Classical economics as put forth by Say, Ricardo, and Mill. Classical economists denied that a level of spending in an economy could be too low to purchase the entire full employment output. Say's Law, which stated that "supply creates its own demand," acknowledged that short run downturns in the economy, due to geopolitical events like war, were possible. However, when these reductions in AD occurred, there would be an eventual adjustment in lower price, wage, and interest rate levels (figure 3-6) that would return the economy to full employment. These events would stimulate an expansion in consumer and investment spending, thus increasing AD and leading to a self-correcting view of the business cycle.

Figure 3-6   Inelastic (Long-Run) Supply Classical Macroeconomic Theory LRAS = NRU

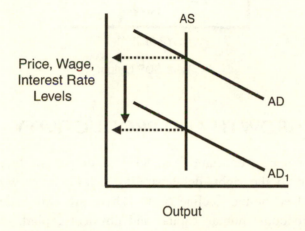

OPERATING BEYOND THE LRAS

Let's view this economic event in a slightly different manner (see figure 3-7). Assume that in the short–run, AS can operate beyond the LRAS (i.e., worker overtime) point A output Y2, due to a heightened determinant of demand, such as consumers anticipating future interest rate hikes so they go on a buying spree. If this economy were operating beyond the NRU (sustainable GDP output level) upward cost pressure on supply inputs would occur as a rationing limit. This will eventually cause the SRAS (unsustainable) curve to shift upward from AS1 to AS2, and will result in a return to real GDP equilibrium at point B Y1, the full employment level.

Figure 3-7 Elastic (Short-Run) Supply LRAS = NRU

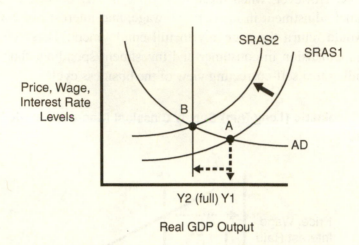

ECONOMIC GROWTH AND PRODUCTIVITY

The LRAS is not at a constant fixed level of output. In fact, the LRAS may shift outward to the right, demonstrating economic growth or inward to the left, should economic decline occur. There are two main sources of economic growth/decline: human capital and physical capital. Investment in human capital would shift LRAS to the right if there was an improvement in skill levels due to heightened education and training. Physical capital investment in research and development may result in improved technology, causing increased efficiency. An economy may experience population growth due to social factors or immigration. Finally, the discovery of new resource inputs or alternative resources may result in increased output capacity. Of course, should these factors operate in the opposite direction, economic shrinkage would result. Therefore, it is easy to see why policies that encourage economic growth (another mission given to the Federal Reserve by Congress) are so vital to a nation's economic well-being. The seeds of controversy, however, are once again sown in a situation where the Federal Reserve's mission (full employment and economic growth) may be in conflict.

John Maynard Keynes, in his book *General Theory of Employment, Interest, and Money* (1936), developed the AE ideas. He pointed out that not all income need be spent at the time it is produced; in fact, it may be saved. Business investment spending is volatile, and a decline in consumption and investment will cause a decrease in total expenditure. This decline in spending causes a buildup of inventories that producers respond to by firing workers and reducing their output. Furthermore, in stark contrast to the Classical economists' assertions, the resulting recessions are not self-correcting and may continue long-term. In other words, an economy can get "stuck" at a very low level of output. Finally, in direct opposition to the classical "laissez faire" view, Keynes believed that government should play the key role in revitalizing a stagnant economy by stimulating demand. This method of government regulation of the business cycle has come to be called *demand-side economics.*

In the 1980s under President Reagan, some economists united to revisit Say's Law. These "supply-siders" advocated the use of tax cuts, deregulation, and privatization as a method of restoring rapid economic growth. They argued that marginal tax rates were so high that they removed the incentive to work, save, and (most importantly) invest in capital goods to increase the aggregate supply. Excessive government regulation of corporate behavior further dampened the incentive to grow business through investment in capital goods. The Laffer curve (figure 3-8) demonstrates the relationship between tax rates and government revenue, and counters the argument that higher tax rates generate more tax revenue. Also remember that taxes are viewed as a leakage in AE theory, which diminishes output. As less capital is available for investment, previously discussed economic growth would be slowed. The argument will be made by supply siders that a low-tax environment promotes economic growth.

Figure 3-8   Laffer Curve

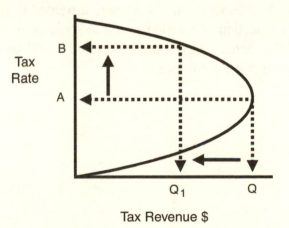

Tax Revenue $

Notice that if the tax rate moves above A to B, tax revenues diminish from Q to Q1. This theory suggests that if tax rates were higher than A, a tax rate cut would not only increase AE total output (aggregate supply would shift right as economic growth results), but actually increase government revenues. Critics suggest that tax cuts are not absolute in their positive effect; that they can be inflationary if undertaken when at or near full employment; and that determination of where you are on the Laffer curve is impossible. Finally, tax cuts may result in budget deficits, causing government borrowing, which raises interest rates and crowds out some private investment. (Crowding out is detailed later in relation to fiscal policy.)

FOCUS ON CONSUMER EXPENDITURE

The majority of expenditure in the U.S. economy (around two-thirds) is by household consumers. Consumers may spend or save their disposable (after-tax) income. Therefore, an understanding of consumer behavior is critical to any attempt to effect a change in the state of the overall economy. John Maynard Keynes provided the following analysis. His theory forms the basis of the "Keynesian" view of a general free market economy and dominated U.S. fiscal policy for more than 50 years. A key element of this general theory on economics was that Keynes believed it possible to measure the spending reaction of consumers with a change in disposable income. This is termed the *marginal propensity to consume/save* (MPC/MPS). Consumers have an equilibrium point for their disposable income (DI) relative to their expenditures. Any point of income above this equilibrium will result in a portion of income being saved. Any point below equilibrium will cause consumers to dissave (exhaust money capital or borrow). In conclusion, if government wanted to stimulate spending by consumers, a reduction of taxation would at some point increase spending. Still, not all of the increase in disposable income would be spent. Figure 3-9 helps us understand this key concept.

Figure 3-9 Marginal Propensity to Consume or Save

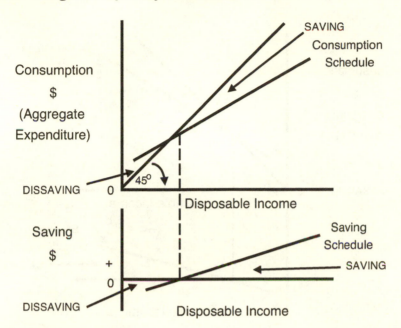

The bisection of the right angle (the 45° line) represents a direct relationship between income and expenditure. In other words, every extra dollar of disposable income received will result in that dollar being expended. The slope of the bisection line is 1. Remember, the formula for the calculation of slope is:

$$\frac{\text{change in vertical}}{\text{change in horizontal}}$$

Therefore, if you determine the slope of actual consumption, you would determine what percentage of income a consumer would spend. The remainder,

$$(1 - \text{MPC}) = \text{MPS}$$

is the marginal propensity to save. For example, the marginal propensity to consume would be

$$\frac{\text{change in expenditure}}{\text{change in disposable income}} = \frac{15}{20} \text{ or } 0.75 \text{ (slope)}$$

This means that for every $1.00 of increased income over equilibrium, $0.75 would be spent by consumers, and therefore, $0.25 would be saved. For every $1.00 of income lost below equilibrium, $0.25 would be dissaved (1 − 0.75 = 0.25 MPS). This formula is applied and shown in figure 3-10.

Figure 3-10   Marginal Propensity to Consume or Save

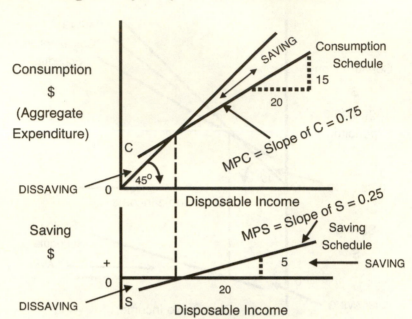

In conclusion, this theory is significant if one wanted to predict the effect that a change in disposable income would have on expenditure. So, if the federal government reduced taxes, DI would increase, increasing expenditure and stimulating expansion of the overall economy. Economic indicators, such as the University of Michigan's consumer sentiment index, attempt to provide economists with insight into the direction of consumer behavior.

BUSINESS INVESTMENT, INCLUDING GOVERNMENT, AND NET EXPORTS TO THE AE MODEL (INJECTIONS AND LEAKAGES)

Remember that consumer spending (C) is not the only component of AE. Businesses also spend money on investment goods (I_g). Furthermore, government (G) spends money through its annual budgets, and foreign economies spend on our exports. An increase in any of the four components would shift the AE upwards. Just as spending increases cause an upward shift of the AE, leakages (savings, taxes, and imports) of the components would result in a downward shift of AE.

Figure 3-11   Marginal Propensity to Consume or Save

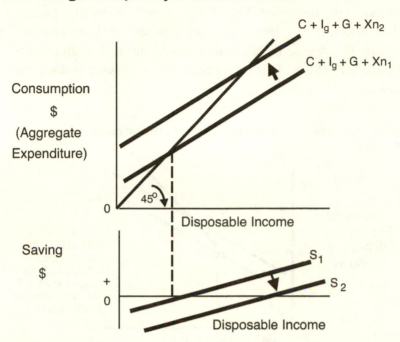

Notice that an increased spending injection in any of the four components of AE results in a movement upward of the entire AE, and a new equilibrium level. Furthermore, since C(MPC) + S(MPS) must equal 1, an upward shift of AE (figure 3-11) must have an equal shift downward of S, and vice versa. Since all four components may be increasing or decreasing at the same time, a leakage and injection analysis would allow one to predict the net effect of changes in AE on GDP output. This analysis is often expressed algebraically. For example, if consumption (C) increased by $5 billion, business investment (I) remained the same, government spending (G) increased by $5 billion, and imports (M) increased by $5 billion, there would be a net increase in the AE of $5 billion:

$$C + I_g + G + Xn = AE = \$5 + \$0 + \$5 - \$5 = \$5$$

This change in AE would then be subject to the multiplier, and a new equilibrium GDP would result. As seen in figure 3-12, if the MPS were 0.25 (resulting in a multiplier of 4), then a net injection in AE of $5 billion would result in equilibrium GDP increasing by $20 billion. If the injection described above occurred, and equilibrium GDP was at the $450 billion level, the new equilibrium level would be $470 billion (5 × 4, the multiplier, = 20). What complicates the injection leakage analysis of AE changes (and thus the resulting impact on equilibrium GDP output) is the fact that the leakage of government taxes upon the consumption component are first subject to the MPC/MPS, prior to being subject to the multiplier. This is due to the fact that if a lump sum tax is imposed upon consumers, they would not just reduce their spending, but also their savings. The degree to which they would make this adjustment is determined by the MPC/MPS. This balanced budget gap issue is discussed later, in fiscal policy.

Figure 3-12   Change in Equilibrium GDP and Investment

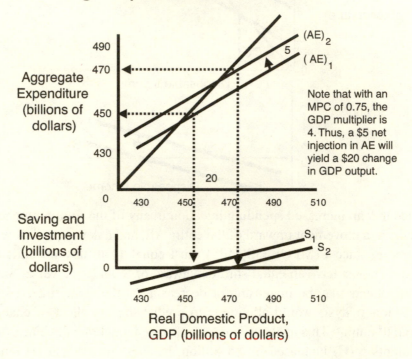

Note that with an MPC of 0.75, the GDP multiplier is 4. Thus, a $5 net injection in AE will yield a $20 change in GDP output.

FOCUS ON I_g AND DISEQUILIBRIUM

A key component of private spending in the AE is gross business investment. This consists of purchased capital goods, inventories, and services that grow the total output (AS) of the economy. The AE model helps to explain how firms react to levels of GDP output greater than and less than equilibrium level (where all production is consumed). In figure 3-13, we see how firms had planned on an investment of $20 billion ($I_{g1}$). However, at the $490 GDP output level, consumers spent less and saved more than firms expected (S$25 > $I_g$$20), as seen by the AE $(C + I_g)_1$. The firms had an increase in their inventories, since consumer spending is insufficient at the GDP output of $490 to sell all of the output produced. When this occurs, firms will lay off workers (lessening total income) and reduce their investment in inventories (contraction of the economy) until GDP equilibrium is attained. Conversely, if AE is greater than GDP output ($S < I_g$), firms will end up with an unplanned decrease in inventory. They will hire workers (increasing total income) and increase output until equilibrium is achieved (expansion of the economy). The AE model serves us well in demonstrating this economic concept, and further reveals the dynamics of the business cycle.

Figure 3-13   Disequilibrium GDP and Investment

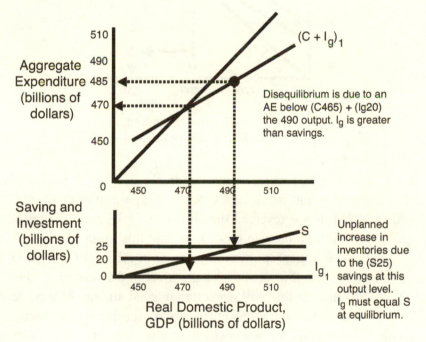

GDP AND THE MULTIPLIER

Since we now are aware of the effect that changes in the components of AE have on GDP equilibrium, we must explain why a change in AE leads to a larger change in GDP. A concept known as the *multiplier* helps us to determine the exact ratio of change relationship between changes in AE and GDP. The multiplier formula is:

$$\text{Multiplier} = \frac{\text{change in read GDP}}{\text{initial change in spending}}$$

The AE model demonstrates the multiplier graphically (figure 3-14).

Figure 3-14   Change in AE and the GDP Multiplier

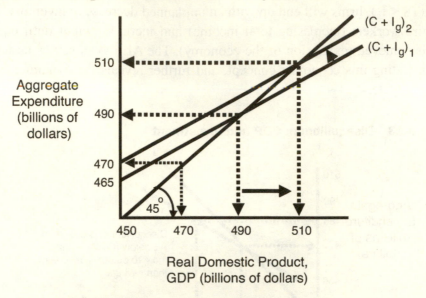

If $(C + I_{g1})$ to $(C + I_{g2})$ represented an increase in I_g of $5 billion ($465 to $470), that increase would result in a change in equilibrium GDP of $20 billion ($490 to $510). If we reversed the shift in $C + I_g$, a $5 billion decrease would cause a $20 billion drop in GDP. How can this initial change in investment spending cause a disproportionate change in AE and GDP? The initial change in spending sets off a spending chain effect in the economy. Remember, the initial investment spending will generate an equal amount of income that is then subject to the MPC and MPS. Furthermore, the initial consumer spending is another household's income, which is also subject to the MPS/MPC. This cycle repeats itself until the money is exhausted. This money is exhausted when a savings of $5 billion is created, equal to the $5 billion increase in investment spending. There is a relationship between the MPS and the multiplier. If the MPS is 0.25, income would have to increase 4 times more than the savings rate to be equal. So, to save $5 billion, $20 billion of income would have to be available. In other words, the multiplier formula is:

$$\frac{1}{\text{MPS}}, \ so \ \frac{1}{0.25} = 4 \quad or \quad \frac{1}{1 - \text{MPC}}, \ so \ \frac{1}{1 - 0.75} = 4$$

The multiplier helps us to understand why a small change in investment can lead to a larger change in equilibrium GDP. The multiplier shows us the impact of investment on business activity. The larger the MPC, the more income generated by investment will be spent. The larger the MPS, the more income leaks into savings and the more the effect of investment is decreased.

IDM, NOMINAL AND REAL INTEREST RATES, AND LOANABLE FUNDS

What governs investment demand? Businesses are profit-maximizing by nature. So, any investment expenditure is governed by the real expected rate of return (notice the use of the word *real*—inflation expectation is significant in this determination of investment and must be factored into the equation). Nominal interest rate would be an interest rate unadjusted for inflation whereas real interest rate would be nominal minus the expected inflation rate over the life of the loan. If the percentage cost of borrowing money is less than the percentage of net profit returned, then the firm should undertake all profitable investment projects. Conversely, if the return is less than the cost, loss would repel the firm from any investment venture. Therefore, firms are sensitive to any excessive anticipated inflation or deflation. Moreover, taxation, technological innovation, household debt, consumer sentiment, producer prices, political climate, interest rates, currency exchange rates, money supply, and stock value also affect a firm's investment expenditure plans. These factors (determinants) cause a shift in a firm's investment demand. The relationship of investment demand (Id) to interest rate (i) and investment quantity is depicted in a very important model (figure 3-15). Notice the direct relationship between real interest and money invested. Suppose that Congress cut corporate taxes by 20%. What would happen to the Id for money?

Figure 3-15   Investment Demand Shifts

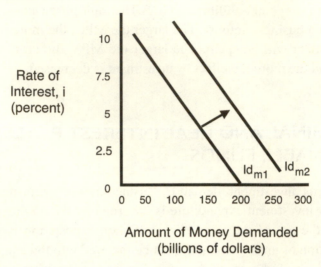

Amount of Money Demanded
(billions of dollars)

The shift in demand for money would cause firms to borrow more money as long as the increase in real rates doesn't exceed the increase in net profits. Because their profit would increase by the reduction of tax, investment would be more desirable.

Another factor at work on Ig is the supply of funds in the loanable funds market (figure 3-16). In a closed economy S = Ig, and in an open economy S = national savings + foreign capital inflow. There are many different financial markets in the financial system: bank deposits, loans, bonds (government and corporate), the stock and commodities markets, to name a few. Savings are free to flow between these various markets (although some may have a cost for liquidation such as an early withdrawal penalty) and individual investors constantly reassess the risk versus reward equation to determine their investment balance (diversification = a blend of many of the asset classes). There is also a value to cash as it is immediately spendable. Other assets, such as real estate, must be converted to cash (liquidity) and the time factor involved is a relevant cost. Based on the market in figure 3-16, $150 billion dollars will be lent and borrowed at an interest rate of 7.5%. Lenders would be willing to bring more money to market if rates rose above 7.5% and less if rates fell below (impacting values in the other financial markets). Conversely, quantity demanded would increase if rates dropped and decrease if rates rose. This relationship between interest rates and investment demand will later become a critical component of fiscal and monetary policy. If you control the money supply, you could affect interest rates and thus encourage or discourage Id, thereby growing or contracting the AE/AD, and AS. Thus, these various outcomes would affect total real GDP, income, job creation, price levels (inflation), currency exchange rates, and economic growth. All of these factors weigh heavily on investors, and monitoring all of this information is of vital importance.

Figure 3-16   Loanable Funds Market

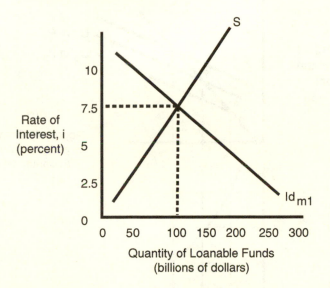

AGGREGATE DEMAND/AGGREGATE SUPPLY MODEL

The AD/AS model represents variable price levels relative to changes in output, employment, and income as aggregate demand and aggregate supply equilibrium occurs. The AD curve is determined by the AE equilibrium at various levels of output, as previously described. The AD curve is downward sloping, revealing the effect that inflation/deflation has on spending. The determinants mentioned earlier, viz.:

- change in consumer spending (C)
- change in gross business investment (I_g)
- change in government spending (G)
- change in net export (X_n)

with respect to AE shifts, result in similar shifts of AD. A leftward shift of AD represents decreased spending; a rightward shift indicates increases at all levels. See figure 3-17.

Figure 3-17   Deriving the Aggregate Demand Curve

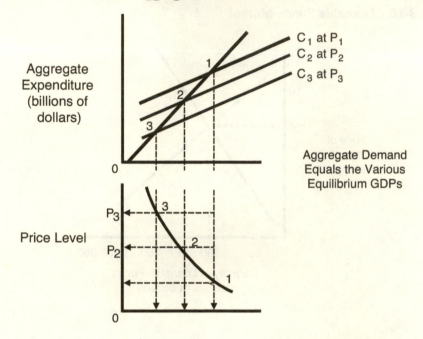

The AS curve represents the various levels of output that businesses will produce at various price levels. Many economists draw the AS curve with three distinct stages: horizontal, transitional, and vertical. Each stage represents a different degree of employment, with horizontal meaning low levels of employment, transitional showing that we are nearing full employment, and vertical signifying full employment (as defined earlier). The transitions from each stage depict the increasing cost of inputs as one nears maximum productivity. Aggregate supply is subject to determinants (such as taxation input costs, expectations, and productivity) that may cause it to shift. A leftward shift of AS_1 to AS_3 would represent increased costs per unit of production. A rightward shift from AS_1 to AS_2 would be a decreased cost per unit of production, due to increased productivity. This is shown in figure 3-18.

Figure 3-18   Changes in Aggregate Supply

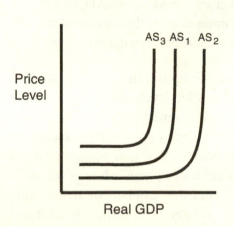

Determinants of Supply
_____

1. Change in input prices
   − Domestic resource availability
     • Land
     • Labor
     • Capital
     • Entrepreneurial ability
   − Prices of imported resources
   − Market power
2. Change in productivity
3. Change in legal institutional environment
   − Business taxes and subsidies
   − Government regulations

The relationship of aggregate demand and aggregate supply reveals the current state of the economy. The model in figure 3-19 depicts various outcomes of shifts in AD/AS.

Figure 3-19   The Equilibrium Price Level Real GDP

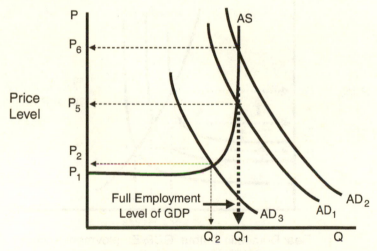

Real Domestic Output, GDP, Employment, Income

Notice that at AD_1/AS equilibrium, there is some rise in price levels, but maximum GDP, employment, and income are achieved. Yet if AD_1 increases to AD_2, the economy cannot produce more g/s to meet that demand. This would result in the rapid increase in price levels that we termed *hyperinflation*. Also, if AD decreased, from AD_1 to AD_3, deflation would result, unemployment would occur, and the GDP would fall. Notice that the model depicts our definition of contraction/recession in the business cycle. If we reversed the AD, from AD_3 to AD_1, we would have an economy in expansion. If AD intersected in the horizontal stage of AS, there could be an increase in GDP without an increase in the price level.

In figure 3-20, we see the possible shifts in AS. Notice that as AS contracted from AS_3 to AS_2, we would experience higher price levels (P_1 to P_2), while at the same time levels of GDP, employment, and income would have decreased (Q_3 to Q_2). As mentioned earlier, this is termed *stagflation* by many economists. Conversely, if an economy's AS grew from AS_1 to AS_3, that economy would be experiencing productivity growth that would lower prices while at the same time increasing GDP, employment, income, and the standard of living. This latter example explains much of our recent prosperity. Also realize that AD and AS can both be moving at the same time, compounding the rate of expansion or contraction. For example, if you had an economy in which AD was increasing while AS was contracting, the rate of inflation would be magnified.

Figure 3-20   Shifts in Aggregate Supply

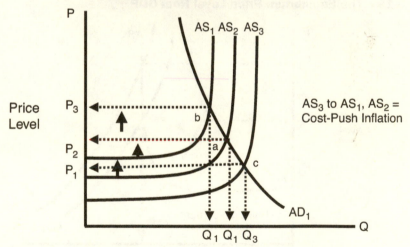

Real Domestic Output, GDP, Employment, Income

AD/AS AND FISCAL POLICY

The Aggregate Expenditure model when used in conjunction with the AD/AS model helps us understand demand-pull and cost-push inflation, as well as recessions and expansions in the business cycle. Since the advent of the

Keynesians during the Great Depression of the 1930s, the federal government has become increasingly responsible for, and thus involved in, managing our economy's well-being. The U.S. government's fiscal policy has, since the 1930s, worked to create full employment, price stability, and economic growth, with varying degrees of success. What is the rationale behind such behavior, and why do many economists question its effectiveness?

When equilibrium AE is inside LRAS, AE1 (c), a recessionary gap is said to be present, as seen in figure 3-21. Angle acb would equal the recessionary gap generating AD/AS equilibrium **d and real GDP Yrg**. Should equilibrium AE occur beyond LRAS, AE2 (e), an inflationary gap exists. Angle gea would equal the inflationary gap generating AD/AS equilibrium **f and real GDP Yig**. If equilibrium AE is at LRAS, AE (a), then an economy is said to be at its full potential and would require no government action. Recall that Classical theory suggests that surplus/shortage of workers and inputs results in lower prices/higher prices, shifting AD, and causing gaps to disappear of their own accord. Keynesian theory counters that an economy can get stuck at low levels of output, requiring government intervention.

Figure 3-21 Recessionary and Inflationary Gaps

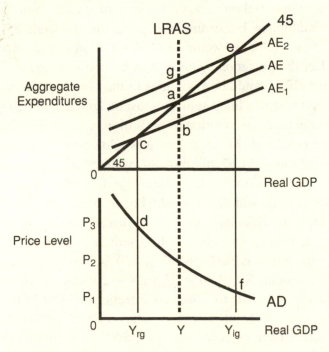

Fiscal policy consists of two basic powers held by the U.S. Congress (subject to approval by the president): taxation and budgetary action spending. Both tend to be structured annually, and may be discretionary (changeable targeted funding) or nondiscretionary (automatic stabilizers) in nature. Policy has two basic directions: expansionary or contractionary. In expansionary fiscal policy, the government is attempting to stimulate the AD by cutting taxes and raising spending levels, or some combination of the two (thereby incurring deficit). In contractionary policy, the government would act to retard the AD through tax increases and spending cuts (thereby incurring surplus). If focused on the consumer, the policy is viewed as (Keynesian) demand-side. If it is focused on business investment, then it is considered (Reaganomics) supply-side.

Equal increases in government taxes and spending result in an increase in GDP output. In other words, if government increased spending by $10 billion and levied a $10 billion lump sum tax, the net effect would be stimulative to the economy by a factor of 1, or $10 billion. Tax cuts/increases are first subject to the MPS/MPC, so tax increases must be larger than spending increases (tax cuts must be larger than spending decreases) to have no effect on the economy's output. This is due to the fact that government spending is subject to the full multiplier, whereas tax cuts are not. To determine the net effect of fiscal policy, one must account for the initial increase or decrease of savings from tax cuts/hikes, then apply the multiplier. For example, if government spends $5 billion (with an MPC of 0.75 the multiplier would be 4), $20 billion would be added to GDP. In order to offset this injection, a lump sum tax with an equal effect must be levied, or the net effect would be a stimulus to the economy. Thus, a $20 billion decrease in GDP through a lump sum tax must be levied. For the tax cut to have a net negative effect on consumption of $5 billion, a tax of $6.67 billion would be required, since 0.25 of the tax payment would come from reduced savings ($0.25 \times \$6.67$ billion = $1.67 billion). So by increasing taxes by $6.67 billion—MPS of $1.67 billion = $5 billion—you would offset the spending injection of $5 billion, and there would be no change in the GDP output. If using the MPC to calculate the size of tax necessary to offset government spending, a simple formula can be used: $X \times MPC$ = the zero effect tax. Assuming the MPC is 0.80, to offset $20 billion of government spending, one would calculate $X \times 0.80 = 20$, so $X = 20/0.80$. Thus, X would equal $25 billion. In other words, to offset an injection of $20 billion of government spending, you would have to levy a tax of $25 billion. Remember, at GDP equilibrium, injections equal leakages; Savings + Taxes + M(Imports) = I_g + G + X(Exports).

FISCAL POLICY ISSUES

Some economists advocate government spending as the most direct way to influence the AD. However, what the money gets spent on is a matter of enormous and heated debate. Is government too large and expensive, or are social needs going unmet? Also, the outcome of a tax cut to consumers is unpredictable because it is unclear how much will actually get spent or saved. Tax cuts to business may result only in more profits and not in increased productivity. Serious questions may be raised as to whether tax cuts/increases should be marginal in nature or across the board, by percentage (progressive) or a dollar amount (regressive). Some are concerned that the rich get richer, while others fear that money goes to those who have not earned it. Finally, consider the political implications of an elected official advocating increased taxes and a reduction in government spending programs!

In light of all the issues merely touched on here, it is easy to see why the U.S. government has run annual deficits for decades and accumulated a national debt. Should government accumulate cyclical deficits and pay down debt during years of surplus? How do we finance these deficits? Are politicians capable of recognizing the need for action? Can opposing parties write legislation in time to be effective? How long does it take for laws to be put into action? Many economists have noticed that by the time an expansionary fiscal policy is constructed and put into place, the state of the economy is such that the policy is not only no longer necessary, but may in fact be counterproductive. If it takes 10 months to construct and implement a fiscal policy and a recession lasts 6 months, how effective is the policy?

CROWDING OUT

One of the most fundamental criticisms of fiscal policy concerns the effect that deficit spending has on interest rates. If government funds a deficit by borrowing money, then, by the nature of money markets, the price (interest rate) of money must increase. As the price of money increases (as was noted earlier with regard to AE), investment demand would further weaken, as would interest-sensitive consumer sectors such as housing and automobiles (durable goods). Therefore, any government injection is offset by a reduction in the AE components of $C + I_g$. In terms of the foreign component of AE, if a government seeks money and interest rates increase, foreign capital will be attracted to the United States. This would cause demand for U.S. dollars to increase, and the dollar would appreciate relative to foreign capital. As the dollar appreciated, U.S. goods would become more expensive to the foreign sector and exports would drop. As the dollar appreciated, foreign goods would become cheaper; thus a greater $-X_n$ would further reduce the AE and counteract the U.S. government's expansionary fiscal policy. This can be expressed in terms of the AD/AS model in figure 3-22.

Figure 3-22   Expansionary Fiscal Policy and Crowding Out

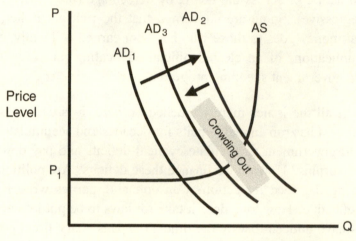

Real GDP (billions), Employment, Income

Notice that if the economy were operating in recession at AD_1, and fiscal policy attempted to stimulate the AD_1 to move to AD_2, crowding out would work to counteract the stimulus package and only move the economy to AD_3. Some economists do not believe that the crowding-out effect is that great, as tax cuts may increase profit and stimulate firms to increase investment demand due to greater expectations. Therefore, firms would be willing to borrow money even at the higher interest rates. Also, the Federal Reserve (as we will see in the section on monetarism) could increase the money supply, thereby keeping interest rates from rising, so there would be no crowding out. Finally, some economists observe that tax cuts to consumers tend to effect only a short-run increase in AD that may be inflationary. Demand-siders criticize supply-siders on the bases that the tax-cut incentive to save, invest, and work harder is not very intense, and that tax cuts tend to have long-run effects on growing the AS. These criticisms do not negate the need to consider the economic impact of these variables when constructing fiscal policy.

AD/AS AND MONETARY POLICY

We have already established the importance that money plays in the free market system. A stable money system, and the need for a central bank to manage that system, are accepted as axioms by economists today. In light of the shortcomings of fiscal policy in managing the state of the economy, can we find better management in the Federal Reserve System? Critical to understanding the role of the "Fed" in managing today's economy is an understanding of money and banking.

MONEY

Money serves three key functions in the free market economy:

1. It is a medium of exchange usable for buying and selling g/s.

2. It is a unit of measure defining price.

3. It is a store of value that preserves wealth for later use.

There are several different measures of the money supply, each offering a slightly different insight. As you will see, the investment demand for money relative to the money supply is key to setting interest rates and influencing AE, AD, and the state of the business cycle.

- M_1 = currency and demand deposits

- M_2 = currency, demand deposits, and near money (money market funds, savings accounts, and certificates of deposit of less than $100,000)

- M_3 = all of the above plus time deposits of more than $100,000 (recently discontinued)

One of the key differences between the different money measurements is the issue of liquidity. *Liquidity* refers to the ease with which an asset can be changed into currency. Stocks and bonds are fairly liquid. Credit cards are not really money, but rather are preapproved loans that are easily accessed. Without question, if you were charged with influencing consumption, the existence of credit cards would complicate your job. Note that the Fed is responsible for maintaining effective control over the money supply; to do so, it focuses on stabilizing the value of money.

Let's revisit the investment demand model (shown in figure 3-23) to review the relationship between money supply and investment demand. If the money supply increased from Ms_1 to Ms_2, interest rates (i) would decrease from 7.5% to 2.5% and the quantity of money borrowed for business investment into capital goods would grow ($150 billion to $250 billion). This increase in gross business investment would increase the AE, shift the AD to the right, and should in the long run grow the AS, due to increased productivity, shifting it to the right.

Figure 3-23   The Money Market

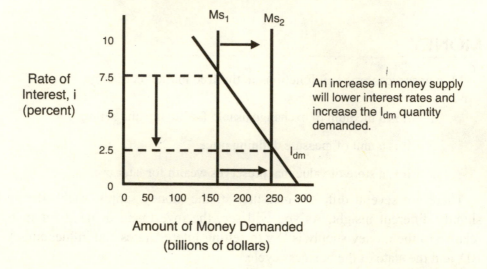

You may recall that in the previously discussed loanable funds market (see figure 3-16) the supply of money was shown as an upward sloping curve rather than perfectly inelastic as in the money market model (figure 3-23). These seemingly irreconcilable differences are not, as there are links between the two markets. The money market depicts the absolute money supply (liquidity preference model) that can be regulated by the Federal Reserve's open market operations and its power to create or destroy money. Should the FOMC choose to lower short-term interest rates it would pay for the purchase of treasury bills from banks by increasing their reserves on deposit with the Fed, an accounting stroke on a computer. The fall in interest rates and increase in quantity demanded Ig is then subject to the multiplier effect causing an increase in real GDP and savings in the loanable funds market that would match the money market rates (figure 3-24).

Figure 3-24 Short-Run Interest Rates

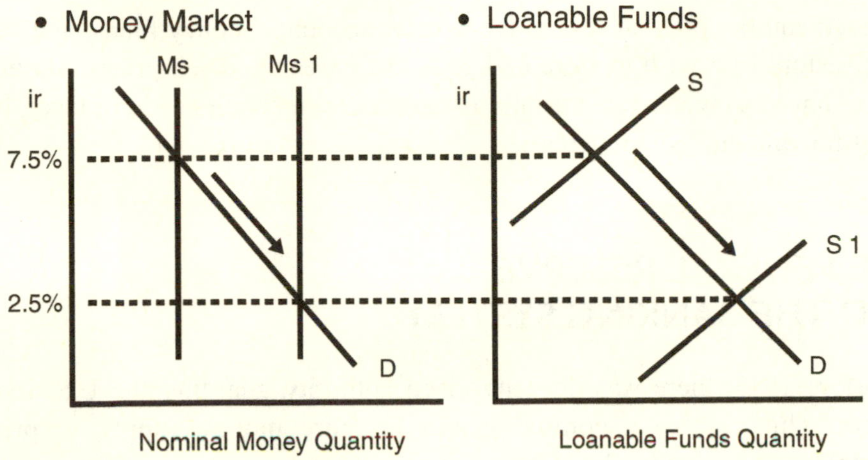

Money Market — Loanable Funds

Nominal Money Quantity — Loanable Funds Quantity

BONDS

Bonds play a key role in manipulating the money supply. Money acts as a storehouse of wealth; however, over time any increase in inflation will diminish the value of the stored currency. Furthermore, because others (home buyers through banks, for example) want to borrow your money, they are willing to pay interest to you for its use. Bonds are also a means of storing wealth. In general, a bond is a promissory note, which obligates the borrower to repay the debt's principal and interest at a specific date in the future (the maturity date). Bonds and the money supply tend to have an inverse relationship. When the money supply decreases, the supply of bonds increases, causing bond prices to drop and interest rate yield to increase. For example (using simple rather than compound interest), a $1,000 bond yields $50 of interest at the end of one year. Your interest rate of return would be 50/1,000 = 5%. If the supply of bonds increased and the price of the bond fell to $667, then the interest rate would be $50/667 or 7.5%. (Note that if overall prices are rising, this inflation would deter households from holding currency, which is depreciating in worth). There are many different types of bonds, but for our purposes there are two main kinds: U.S. Government Treasury bonds and corporate bonds. These bonds compete for investors' stored assets. Generally, U.S. Treasuries are viewed as more secure than corporate bonds and thus they tend to yield a lower rate of return. Also, recall the concept of "crowding out," which was covered earlier.

STOCK EQUITIES

Stock equities offer an alternative to bank accounts, money funds, and bonds for investors who wish to store and grow their wealth. Stock prices and bonds tend to have an inverse relationship. In general, when equities are in favor, bond prices fall and their yield increases.

THE FEDERAL RESERVE AND THE BANKING SYSTEM

Before 1913, there was no centralized authority guarding the U.S. money system. This created a confusing and insecure money supply of private banknotes. These unregulated banks were at times mismanaged (sometimes criminally so) and sparked runs (panics) on banks, as the management's loss of depositors' assets became known. These speculatory investments by bankers contributed to severe market expansions and contractions, as evidenced by the Knickerbocker Trust case in 1907. The Panic of 1907, triggered by the losses incurred by copper market speculation of the Knickerbocker Trust president and his associates, provided the necessary impetus for Congress to act. The Federal Reserve System, established by Congress in 1913, holds power over the money and banking system. Its Board of Governors has 7 members, appointed by the president for staggered 14-year terms. It is the central controlling authority for the system and its power means that the system operates like a central bank. Two sets of bodies assist the Board:

1. The Federal Open Market Committee (FOMC) includes the seven governors plus five regional Federal Reserve Bank presidents, whose terms alternate. They set policy on the buying and selling of government bonds, the most important type of monetary policy.

2. The Federal Advisory Council includes 12 prominent commercial bankers, one from each Fed district, who act as advisors to the Board.

The country is divided into 12 districts, each with its own Federal Reserve Bank and 2 or 3 branch banks. The districts implement the basic directives of the Board of Governors. Each is semi-public, owned by member banks but controlled by the Federal Reserve Board. They act as bankers' banks by accepting reserve deposits and making loans to banks and other financial institutions. The Fed serves many functions, both regulatory and supervisory. Its main purpose is to regulate the supply of money and maintain price stability. The Fed is an independent agency. Its directors, appointed by the president and confirmed by the Senate, have lengthy terms to insulate them from political pressure by elected officials.

TYPES OF BANKS

Commercial banks are privately owned institutions. They consist of state banks (two-thirds of the national total) and national banks (chartered by the federal government). Thrift institutions are regulated by the Treasury Department but are subject to the monetary control of the Fed. They consist of savings and loan associations, mutual savings banks, and credit unions (which are owned by depositors and are run as nonprofit banks). Recent laws have loosened the limitations on the services that banks can offer. The Financial Services Modernization Act of 1999 allows mergers that may well consolidate most financial services, including insurance, within one firm. This consolidation of financial services is taking place globally as well.

BANKS, LOANS, AND THE MONEY MULTIPLIER

One of the three main powers of the Fed is the ability to set the reserve ratio requirement for banks. This power allows a type of banking known as *fractional reserve banking*. This simply means that banks, by law, must put a set percent of their total deposits on reserve with the Fed. For a bank to operate legally, it must maintain a balance between its assets (owned value) and its liabilities (owed value). A simple, typical balance sheet would look like figure 3-25.

Figure 3-25 Balance Sheet of a Commercial Bank

ASSETS		=	LIABILITIES	
Cash	$ 0			
Excess Reserve	60,000		Demand Deposits	$ 50,000
Property	240,000		Capital Stock	250,000
Total	$300,000		Total	$300,000

Notice that the assets equal the liabilities. What happens when a $50,000 loan is made to a firm that wants to make a capital-good investment? See the changes to the balance sheet in figure 3-26.

Figure 3-26   Balance Sheet of a Commercial Bank

ASSETS	=	LIABILITIES
Cash $ 0		
Excess Reserve 60,000		Demand Deposits $100,000
Loans *50,000*		Capital Stock 250,000
Property 240,000		Total $350,000
Total $350,000		

"New money" in the amount of $50,000 was created. When a bank makes a loan, it creates money. A bank may create as much money as its excess reserves allow. When a loan is created, the money supply increases; when a loan is repaid, the money supply constricts. When the firm repays the loan, the money is destroyed. If the Fed decreases the reserve ratio, more money can be loaned (easy money). If the reserve ratio is increased, less money can be loaned (tight money). Money is borrowed from a bank with the intention of spending it, on g/s by the consumer or on investment goods by firms. What they are spending is another person's income. When people receive income, they deposit that money into a bank, which in turn loans it to another household or firm. This process is the core of the money multiplier. Like the MPS concept, the monetary multiplier is the inverse of the required reserve (1/required reserve ratio). So, if the reserve ratio requirement (a bank's MPS, if you will) is 20%, what is the multiplier? Solution: $1/0.20 = 5$.

If $1,000 is deposited into a bank, $5,000 will be added to the money supply before the deposit-loan-redeposit-reloan cycle runs its course. The money supply, therefore, depends heavily on banks' willingness to loan money. Bankers are subject to determinants of supply, so they may during expansion be overly liberal in loaning and during contraction extremely conservative. Banks thus tend to intensify the business cycle. The Fed plays a key role in countering this tendency, which is why you often hear the Fed referred to as a countercyclical institution. This simply means that when recession occurs, the Fed acts in a way that encourages banks to increase lending, thereby stimulating the economy out of contraction. If the business cycle is overexpanding, the Fed acts to discourage loans, thereby going against the cycle. Why put so much effort into regulating the economy? Simply stated, people prefer an economy that avoids the human suffering present during a recession. The Federal Reserve is charged with the mission to achieve and maintain price stability, full employment, and sustainable economic growth through monetary policy.

THE FED AND MONETARY POLICY

The Fed operates much like the banks mentioned earlier. It too must maintain a balance sheet that is solvent, with assets that equal or exceed liabilities. The Fed's balance sheet consists of loans to commercial banks, reserves of commercial banks, cash (Federal Reserve Notes) reserves, Treasury deposits, and Treasury Bills (government bonds). The purchase and sale of this last item (open market operations) is the main source of monetary policy power. It is the Fed's main policy tool to influence the money supply. This ability to operate in the bond market was confirmed in the Accord of 1951 negotiated between the U.S. Treasury and the most powerful arm of the Federal Reserve System, the Federal Open Market Committee (FOMC). As noted earlier, this group consists of the seven members of the Board of Governors and five regional bank presidents, four of whom rotate on a two-year term (the New York Federal Reserve Bank president is a permanent voting member). Each member has one vote to determine board policy. All bank presidents participate in private discussions, which are published on a delayed basis. Some economists argue that this panel holds the health of the U.S. economy in their hands and thus should be more open to the public. Some even go so far as to say that the FOMC should be replaced by a fixed set of rules that would force them to act in a set way to changes in economic indicators. Most economists counter that the Fed has been very successful in regulating the economy, and point out that tying it to fixed responses may jeopardize our economic well-being.

FOMC

The FOMC meets approximately every six weeks to analyze economic indicators (they publish a "beige book" full of them), gauge the state of the economy, and conclude a "recession watch, neutral, or inflation watch." They announce the federal funds target rate (the rate for overnight borrowing from other banks' reserves), the discount rate (the rate at which banks borrow from the Fed's funds), and direct the New York Federal Reserve Bank to buy/sell government bonds from/to commercial banks and the general public (see the previous section on bonds). This is the most important instrument for influencing the money supply, interest rates, and investment demand. These acts stimulate or constrain the AD, thus influencing prices, GDP, employment, and disposable income.

If inflation is the problem, the Fed sells government bonds to remove money from the economy. This raises interest rates, leading to less investment spending, which in turn lowers AD. Household consumption (C) is indirectly affected as the federal funds rate influences consumer credit rates. Because consumer credit rates are higher than the prime interest rate at which firms borrow, consumer borrowing and spending are negatively impacted. This tightening of the money supply is depicted in figure 3-27.

Figure 3-27 The Money Market and FOMC Sale of Bonds

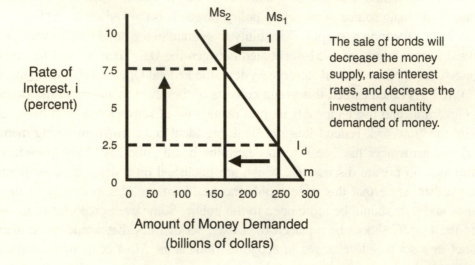

This decrease in money reduces the gross business investment component of AE and shifts the AD to the left. Notice the decreased GDP output, employment, and disposable income in the economy shown in figure 3-28. The decrease in price levels is greatest if the economy is in stage 2 or 3 inflation.

Figure 3-28 Contractory Monetary Policy

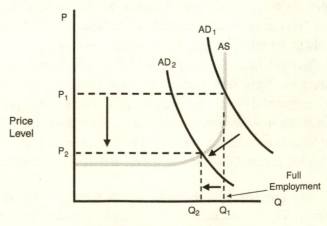

How would the FOMC fight inflation? It should pursue a tight money policy: sell bonds, raise the discount and federal funds rates, and discourage lending and borrowing, thereby reducing gross business investment. The AD would move inward and the economy would contract.

How would the FOMC fight recession? It should pursue an easy money policy: buy bonds, lower the discount and federal funds rates, and encourage lending and borrowing, thereby increasing gross business investment. The AD would move outward and the economy would expand. Figure 3-29 graphs this expansionary monetary policy.

Figure 3-29   Expansionary Monetary Policy

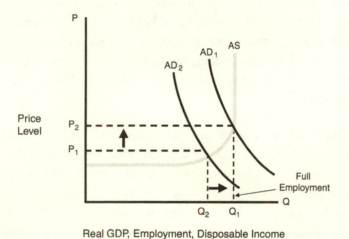

Real GDP, Employment, Disposable Income

IMPACT OF THE GLOBAL ECONOMY

Remember that one of the components of AE is net foreign trade (X_n). World trade has increased globally and is an increasingly significant portion of the U.S. economy. The volume of world trade has increased tremendously since the end of World War II. The United States plays a major role in shaping this trade. Adam Smith's book, *The Wealth of Nations*, points out the advantages of specialization and international trade. They both increase productive efficiency and allow greater total output than would otherwise be possible. Production possibilities tables allow us to quantify the efficiency gains of specialization. This is known as the *principle of comparative advantage*.

NAFTA AND GATT

Three major international agreements have furthered the movement toward a global economy: the 1958 EU, the 1993 NAFTA, and the 1995 Uruguay GATT. The European Union ("common market") comprises 15 European nations. The EU has formed a powerful trade bloc, reducing or eliminating tariffs among its members while at the same time establishing tariffs on g/s from outside. Some U.S. firms have argued that this bloc makes it difficult for them to compete within the EU. One of the most recent, controversial, and significant accomplishments of the EU was the establishment of a common currency, the *euro*.

Somewhat in response to the growing power of the EU, was the 1993 North American Free Trade Agreement, forming a major trade bloc of Canada, Mexico, and the United States. This trade agreement, which was phased in by 2008, established a free-trade zone designed to reduce and eventually eliminate tariffs and other trade barriers among the signatories. Recently, Latin American nations have expressed an interest in expanding the benefits of NAFTA to all of Central and South America.

The 1995 General Agreement on Tariffs and Trade (GATT) established the World Trade Organization (WTO) as a permanent successor to the less formal GATT negotiations. China's recent entrance into the WTO has broadened the reach of the organization to more than 140 nations. Although in some ways incomplete, the WTO provides for some standardization on significant trade issues such as protectionist quotas, subsidies, and trademark, patent, or copyright infringement. Structural resolution of trade disputes is possible in WTO institutions, with approved tariff punishment for violators.

Both the NAFTA and the GATT have proponents as well as critics. Critics are concerned that firms will be able to circumvent U.S. laws that protect workers and the environment. Are labor unions, worker safety laws, minimum wage laws, and environmental protection rules effective if firms can shift production to nations that are weak in these areas? Proponents counter that most of the world's trade is among advanced industrial nations that have well-established worker and environmental protection laws. Adherents argue that as the free flow of g/s raises the output and disposable income levels in poorer nations, the increase in living standards will engender stronger laws, thereby spreading free market benefits across the world.

The new rules have created intense competition between firms. The tendency of firms to survive competition through merger and acquisition has hastened the formation of new multinational companies. These multinationals, as the name implies, produce and distribute g/s globally.

COMPARATIVE ADVANTAGE

The principle of comparative advantage is based on the law of increasing opportunity costs. Opportunity costs reflect the differing levels of inputs and technology present within a country. When two nations are compared as to efficiency of production of certain goods, we can see which total output is the greatest, resulting in the lowest cost. Even though one nation may enjoy absolute advantage over another in the production of goods, it serves both nations' best interests to seek the lower domestic opportunity cost for the less productive nation. This is made clear in the following table of production possibilities (table 3-1).

In this example, notice that Canada has greater total productivity in both apple juice (60) and maple syrup (60) when compared to U.S. apple juice (30) and maple syrup (15). Canada has a cost advantage over the United States in both products. Now what? Should the United States give up all production? Should it make only apple juice, only maple syrup, or some combination? Comparative advantage tells us that the United States should produce its lower domestic opportunity cost product, apple juice. We know this because it must sacrifice 10 units of apple juice to get 5 units of syrup, so 1 unit of apple juice is 0.5 units of syrup. The cost to Canada is greater, as it must give up 1 unit of maple syrup to gain 1 unit of apple juice. The United States should produce apple juice while Canada produces maple syrup. The result is more total apple juice and syrup produced. Canada will produce 60 units of maple syrup and the United States will produce 30 units of apple juice, for a total of 90 units produced. If Canada produced at the B level while the United States produced at the F level, a total of 80 units of goods would be produced. There is a net gain of 10 units of extra produce to be divided between the countries. Both end up with more juice and syrup! The trade exchange rate would end up with Canada wanting 1 unit of syrup for > 1 units of U.S. apple juice. The United States would want to get > 0.5 units of syrup for 1 unit of juice. The actual exchange would be determined by other factors, such as total world demand and supply. If the exchange rate ended up at 1 unit of syrup for 1.6

units of juice, then Canada could keep 45 units of maple syrup (gain of 5; see B column) and trade for 24 (gain of 4) units of apple juice. The United States would keep 6 (gain of 6) units of apple juice and get 15 (same as before at maximum production) units of maple syrup. Notice that both nations have more than if they pursued independent production.

Table 3-1

Canada's production possibilities table (millions of gallons)				
Product	**Production alternatives**			
	A	B	C	D
Apple juice	0	20	40	60
Maple syrup	60	40	20	0
	Total 60			

United States production possibilities table (millions of gallons)				
Product	**Production alternatives**			
	E	F	G	H
Apple juice	0	10	20	30
Maple syrup	15	10	5	0
	Total 20			

FINANCING INTERNATIONAL TRADE

A major stumbling block to trade between nations is the involvement of different national currencies. An American firm exporting a g/s to a Brazilian firm does not want to be paid in Brazilian riales, because that currency cannot be spent in the United States. So, the importer must exchange its currency for U.S. dollars. This service is provided (for a fee) by major banks that have created currency exchanges.

U.S. exports cause an increased demand by Brazilians for U.S. dollars. The increased foreign demand for the U.S. dollar increases the supply of the foreign currency in exchange markets. U.S. imports would increase the demand for the foreign currency and would increase the supply of U.S. dollars in exchange markets. This situation is graphically portrayed in figure 3-30. Notice that as the demand for U.S. dollars increased from D to D_1, the number of riales needed to purchase that dollar increased from 5 to 7.5.

Figure 3-30 The Currency Money Market

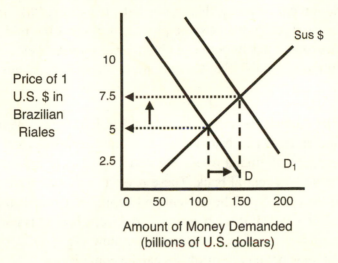

Price of 1
U.S. $ in
Brazilian
Riales

Amount of Money Demanded
(billions of U.S. dollars)

BALANCE OF PAYMENTS

The balance of payments account refers to the sum of a country's transactions with other countries and is summarized in three main accounts: current, capital, and financial account balances. Today, most economists combine the capital and financial accounts (as they are similar in content) into the financial account.

The current account primarily tracks the import and export of goods and services, but also includes net international transfer payments and net international factor income. If a nation imports more than it exports, it has an unfavorable balance of trade/current account deficit. If a nation exports more than it imports, it has a favorable balance of trade/current account surplus. The current account is exports – imports + net investment income (net interest and dividends paid by foreigners to Americans) + net transfers (foreign aid, money sent to Americans or their families living overseas). This account is often termed the "balance of trade" and the U.S. has run deficits in this account for decades. This trade deficit results because the U.S. imports more than it exports.

The economic impact of trade deficits is an oft-debated topic. Is it good or bad for an economy? If a nation imports more than it exports, a net job increase in the foreign nation is created. If there is unemployment at home, it is difficult to justify this "exporting of jobs" (a view of some towards NAFTA and WTO reducing trade barriers). If the demand for foreign goods and services must be paid for in the foreign currency, this causes a depreciation of the net importer's currency (discussed later) that at some point may reverse the trade imbalance. On the positive side a net importer is able to live outside their domestic PPF curve. Also, if the foreign worker's wages are lower, this represents a deflationary effect.

The financial account records trade in assets such as gold, government securities, banking liabilities (deposits/loans), corporate securities, and fixed assets such as real estate. The official reserves account consists of the foreign currencies held by a nation's central bank. These reserves are increased or decreased in reaction to the balance of the current and capital account. If the balance is negative, a deficit is noted; if the balance is positive, a benefit is noted. Whether a deficit or surplus is good or bad depends on how the issue is resolved. The implications of trade deficits or surpluses can be complicated.

THE 2003 U.S. BALANCE OF PAYMENTS

In 2003, the United States exported $714 billion of merchandise and imported $1,263 billion, for a merchandise trade deficit of $549 billion. Service exports, however, were $305 billion and service imports were $246 billion, for a surplus of approximately $59 billion. The trade deficit on goods and services, therefore, was $490 billion. U.S. interest payments to other countries and U.S. interest income from abroad were $250 billion and $272 billion, respectively. There was also a net outflow of $68 billion in unilateral transfers. Therefore, the current account showed an overall deficit of $536 billion.

Capital account transactions yielded a net outflow of $3.1 billion. For the financial account, U.S. investors acquired $277 billion of assets abroad and foreign investors acquired $857 billion of assets in the United States, yielding a net financial and capital account surplus of $580 billion. That surplus, minus a statistical discrepancy of $34 billion, balanced the $536 billion current account deficit.

This is an example of a capital inflow. It allows the United States to run a trade deficit without any impact on the dollar's international value (without the capital inflow the dollar would depreciate). There are many reasons why investors and foreign governments would do this. Some examples are:

1. Investors prefer to save in the U.S. for security reasons.

2. The interest yield may be higher than domestic rates.

3. Capital appreciation is at a higher rate (a U.S. company's growth or profits may be attractive).

4. A country may want to prevent its currency from appreciating.

CURRENCY EXCHANGE RATES

There are two major types of currency exchange formats: floating and fixed, although a managed float is an available option also. At the end of World War II, 44 nations met and created the Bretton Woods system. The U.S. dollar served as the focal point of this system because the U.S. dollar became the reserve currency of the system. Countries bought and sold dollars to maintain their exchange rates. The value of the U.S. dollar was fixed at $35 per ounce of gold and was convertible on demand for foreigners holding U.S. dollars. The dollar became as good as gold.

Two new organizations were also created at the Bretton Woods Conference, the International Monetary Fund and the World Bank. The IMF was created to supervise the exchange-rate practices of member nations. It also was intended to lend money to nations that were unable to meet their payment obligations (that is, to do "bailouts"). IMF funds come from fees charged to the 178 member nations. The World Bank, funded through the sale of bonds, loans money to developing nations for economic development. The Bretton Woods system dissolved in 1971 as the U.S. dollar came under devaluation pressure and gold drained from the nation's reserves. In March 1973, a managed, floating exchange rate was established by the major industrial countries. Central banks of various nations have at times intervened to alter their nation's currency value. An example of this occurred in 1995 when the Fed and U.S. Treasury bought German marks and Japanese yen to increase the value of the dollar, which they thought had fallen excessively. The managed float has withstood severe economic upheaval, such as the OPEC oil crisis in 1973. Some nations, to maintain a more stable domestic currency, have "pegged" the value of their currency to a fixed rate with the U.S. dollar or another industrial nation's currency. An independent floating exchange rate would be subject to the laws of supply and demand in the currency marketplace.

For example, assume that the nation of Argentina imported more g/s from the United States than it exported. The market for the Argentine peso would look like the model in figure 3-31. Notice that as the demand for the U.S. dollar increases, to pay for the imports, the price of the U.S. dollar relative to the Argentine peso increases. In other words, the value of the Argentine peso depreciates while the U.S. dollar appreciates, as seen in figure 3-31.

Figure 3-31   The Currency Money Market

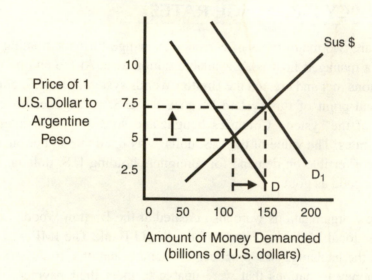

This has significant trade implications. Because of poor management of their government's fiscal/monetary policy, some nations may have to endure a major depreciation of their currency. The impact of depreciation in our example would be a significant reduction in Argentina's ability to import American g/s. At the same time, the cheaper Argentine peso would make its goods cheaper to Americans and should stimulate U.S. demand for Argentine g/s. The impact of currency appreciation/depreciation gives us the main impetus for long-run trade equilibrium. For less industrialized nations that depend on export of farm products and raw materials, currency fluctuations may lead to serious destabilization of the domestic economy. The lack of price stability and increased unemployment resulting from economic contraction in the cycle may result in political upheaval. Over the past several years, the United States has recorded large trade deficits, primarily with Japan and China. At the same time, the U.S. rate of savings has declined to finance these increased imports. Many of these dollars have returned to the United States in the form of greater foreign asset ownership. Those concerned about this trade deficit point to the jobs lost to overseas producers and the loss of U.S. assets to foreign ownership. Others point to the increased standard of living achieved and assert that the foreign assets invested in the United States increase our production capacity, which will create the output necessary to service the foreign debt in the long run. The long-term outcome of this situation is unknown.

PRACTICE TEST 1

CLEP Macroeconomics

Also available at the REA Study Center (*www.rea.com/studycenter*)

This practice test is also offered online at the REA Study Center. Since all CLEP exams are administered on computer, we recommend that you take the online version of the test to receive these added benefits:

- **Timed testing conditions** – Gauge how much time you can spend on each question.
- **Automatic scoring** – Find out how you did on the test, instantly.
- **On-screen detailed explanations of answers** – Learn not just the correct answer, but also why the other answer choices are incorrect.
- **Diagnostic score reports** – Pinpoint where you're strongest and where you need to focus your study.

PRACTICE TEST 1

CLEP Macroeconomics

(Answer sheets appear in the back of the book.)

TIME: 90 Minutes
80 Questions

DIRECTIONS: Each of the questions or incomplete statements below is followed by five possible answers or completions. Select the best choice in each case and fill in the corresponding oval on the answer sheet.

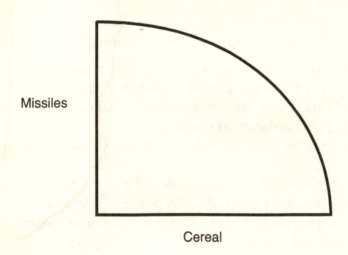

1. Which of the following would cause the production possibilities curve shown above to shift outward?

    (A) Reopening a cereal plant that had been closed
    (B) Rehiring laid-off cereal workers
    (C) Using machinery for missile production instead of cereal production
    (D) Using machinery for cereal production instead of missile production
    (E) Developing a more efficient cereal-making process

2. Which of the following is an example of an economic trade-off?

    (A) A 12% rate of return on an investment
    (B) Reducing unemployment while increasing economic growth
    (C) Increasing the national savings rate while investment spending rises
    (D) Spending less on education programs due to an increase in military spending
    (E) Buying milk and cookies

3. Because resources are _____, trade-offs between alternative uses of those resources must be made.

    (A) available
    (B) scarce
    (C) sold in markets
    (D) tangible
    (E) unlimited

4. Which of the following best describes "efficiency"?

    (A) Spending the least amount of money for an item
    (B) Obtaining the largest possible output from limited resources
    (C) Production of the items that are most in demand
    (D) An equal distribution of scarce resources
    (E) Lowering the price on your goods so that you sell more goods

5. Suppose two countries are each capable of individually producing two given products. Instead, each specializes by producing the good for which it has a comparative advantage and then trades with the other country. Which of the following is most likely to result?

    (A) Both countries will benefit from increased production of goods.
    (B) Unemployment will increase in one country and decrease in the other.
    (C) There will be more efficient production in one country but less efficient production in the other.
    (D) The two countries will become more independent of each other.
    (E) Both countries will be harmed by increased productive inefficiency.

6. Another way to define GDP is as the market value of

    (A) the resource inputs used in the production of output in an economy
    (B) all final goods and services produced in an economy in a given year
    (C) all final and intermediate goods and services produced in a given year
    (D) national income earned by consumers, producers, and exporters
    (E) national income earned by producers and consumers

7. The economic indicator that measures the price change over time, using a fixed market basket of typical goods and services, is the

    (A) producer price index
    (B) consumer sentiment index
    (C) GDP
    (D) CPI
    (E) national income index

8. From an economist's perspective, which of the following is NOT considered to be investment (I_g)?

    (A) Purchasing new computers for the accounting office
    (B) Building a new plant facility
    (C) Buying back outstanding shares of company stock
    (D) Building an office complex
    (E) Increases in the warehouse inventories of finished product

9. The expenditures or output approach to measuring GDP does so by totaling

    (A) spending by employees and businesses on rent, resource inputs, and consumption of fixed capital
    (B) payments to employees, rents, interest, dividends, undistributed corporate profits, proprietors' income, indirect business taxes paid, consumption of fixed capital, and net foreign factor income earned in the United States
    (C) payments to employees, rents, interest, dividends, corporate profits, proprietors' income, and indirect business taxes, and subtracting the consumption of fixed capital
    (D) spending for consumption, investment, net exports, and government purchases
    (E) the total spending for consumption and government purchases, but subtracting public and private transfer payments

10. During the expansion phase of the business cycle

(A) the inflation rate decreases, but productive capacity increases
(B) the inflation rate and productive capacity decrease
(C) employment, income, and output decrease
(D) employment increases, but output decreases
(E) employment, income, and output increase

11. A headline reads: "Auto sales decline and the steel industry suffers a slump; unemployment rises." This type of unemployment can best be characterized in economic terms as

(A) frictional
(B) structural
(C) total unemployment
(D) cyclical
(E) natural

12. Kevin has lost his job in an automobile plant because the company began using robots for welding on the assembly line. Kevin plans to go to technical school to learn how to repair microcomputers. The type of unemployment Kevin is faced with is

(A) frictional
(B) structural
(C) educational
(D) cyclical
(E) natural

13. At the full employment unemployment rate, there is/are only

(A) cyclical and frictional unemployment
(B) downward pressure on wage rates
(C) frictional and structural unemployment
(D) cyclical unemployment
(E) undercounted "discouraged workers" unemployment

AD/AS

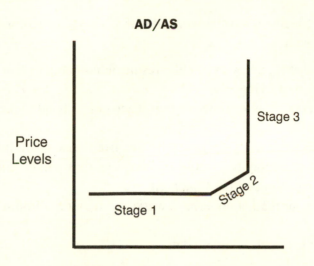

Output, Income, and Employment

14. Refer to the preceding diagram. A decrease in total spending in Stage 2 will

    (A) decrease the price level, but not employment and output
    (B) decrease employment and output, but not the price level
    (C) decrease employment, output, and the price level
    (D) increase employment, output, and the price level
    (E) cause unemployment and inflation

15. Refer to the preceding diagram. An increase in total spending in Stage 3 will increase

    (A) output and decrease price levels
    (B) employment and the price level
    (C) output and the price level
    (D) the price level, but not output or employment
    (E) the price level and decrease the natural rate of unemployment

16. An increase in transportation costs will most likely cause the price level and real GDP to change in which of the following ways?

	Price Level	Real GDP
(A)	increase	increase
(B)	increase	decrease
(C)	increase	no change
(D)	decrease	increase
(E)	decrease	decrease

17. Select the statement most associated with Classical economists that Keynes disagreed with

    (A) A market economy eventually results in monopolies that damage the standard of living.
    (B) Market economies function best when government makes supply decisions.
    (C) Market economies are generally free from price and output cycles.
    (D) A market economy is self-correcting and thus will eventually recover from recession without intervention.
    (E) The factor market underpays workers without minimum wage laws.

18. Based on the circular flow model,

    (A) government plays no role in the flow of goods and services
    (B) households are suppliers in the product market and consumers are suppliers in the factor market
    (C) firms purchase goods in the product market
    (D) households expend their income in the product market and earn their income in the factor market
    (E) firms incur costs in the product market and obtain revenue in the factor market

19. In the aggregate expenditures model, the primary determinant of the level of consumption and saving in the economy is the

    (A) inflation rate
    (B) level of investment
    (C) level of income
    (D) level of prices
    (E) interest rate

20. Consumers purchase bonds, rather than continuing to hold currency, because they believe that interest rates will decline in the future. Such purchases point to which of the following scenarios?

    (A) There has been an upward shift in consumers' marginal propensity to consume
    (B) Consumers expect little need for cash
    (C) Consumers expect the value of currency to appreciate in the short term
    (D) Consumers speculate that currency will depreciate in the future
    (E) Bonds will drop in value relative to currency

21. In a closed private economy, if the interest rate falls, businesses expect expansion of the economy, and as a result the investment demand also rises, then the

(A) expenditure equilibrium will shift downward and GDP will decline
(B) investment schedule and aggregate expenditures schedule will shift upward
(C) investment and aggregate expenditures schedules will shift downward with greater unemployment
(D) investment schedule will shift upward and the aggregate expenditures schedule will shift downward, and output will decrease
(E) investment schedule will shift downward and the aggregate expenditures schedule will shift upward

22. In a closed economy with no government, an increase in autonomous investment of $25 billion increases domestic output from $600 billion to $700 billion. The marginal propensity to consume is

(A) 0.25 and the multiplier is 4
(B) 0.50 and the multiplier is 2
(C) 0.75 and the multiplier is 4
(D) 0.80 and the multiplier is 5
(E) the MPS is 0.75 with a multiplier of 4

23. Other things being equal, if U.S. steel exports fell, the economy would see a(n)

(A) increase in domestic aggregate expenditures and the equilibrium level of GDP
(B) decrease in domestic aggregate expenditures and the equilibrium level of GDP
(C) decrease in government spending and a decrease in GDP
(D) zero effect on domestic GDP, because imports will offset the change in exports
(E) decrease in the marginal propensity to balance trade

24. Leakages from the income-expenditure stream are

(A) consumption, saving, and transfers
(B) investment, spending, and transfer payments
(C) saving, taxes, and transfers
(D) saving, taxes, and imports
(E) imports, taxes, and transfers

25. If a lump-sum tax of $40 billion is levied and the MPS is 0.25, then the saving schedule will shift

    (A) upward by $10 billion
    (B) downward by $160 billion
    (C) upward by $25 billion
    (D) downward by $10 billion
    (E) downward by $25 billion

26. If a government raises its expenditure by $25 billion and at the same time levies a lump-sum tax of $25 billion, the net effect on the economy will be to

    (A) increase GDP by $25 billion
    (B) increase GDP by less than $100 billion, because the multiplier is 4
    (C) increase GDP by more than $50 billion
    (D) increase GDP by $50 billion
    (E) make no change in GDP

Aggregate Expenditure

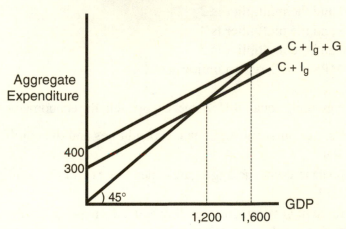

27. Refer to the preceding graph. The size of the multiplier associated with changes in government spending in this economy is

    (A) 2.50
    (B) 3.00
    (C) 5.00
    (D) 6.67
    (E) 4.00

28. Refer to the preceding graph. If this economy is a closed economy without a government sector, the level of GDP would be

(A) $1,200 billion
(B) $200 billion
(C) $300 billion
(D) $1,600 billion
(E) $500 billion

29. As Americans increase their purchase of foreign goods and services, the aggregate expenditure relationship to the aggregate demand and supply model would indicate that a

(A) fall in our aggregate expenditure will cause domestic price level to decrease, aggregate demand to fall, and GDP to decline
(B) fall in our domestic price level will decrease our imports and increase our exports, thereby reducing the net exports component of aggregate demand
(C) fall in our domestic price levels will decrease our imports and reduce unemployment
(D) rise in our domestic price level will increase our imports and reduce our exports, thereby reducing the net exports component of aggregate demand
(E) rise in our domestic price level will decrease our imports and increase our exports, thereby reducing the net exports component of aggregate demand

30. Which combination of factors would most likely increase aggregate demand?

(A) A decrease in consumer debt and an increase in the value of the dollar
(B) An increase in consumer debt and a decrease in foreign demand for products
(C) An increase in the money supply and a decrease in interest rates
(D) An increase in personal taxes and a decrease in government spending
(E) An increase in business taxes and a decrease in corporate earnings

31. If the economy is operating in stage 2, the intermediate range, of aggregate supply, and business investment decreases, then price level, income, and employment would most likely change in which of the following ways?

	Price Level	Income	Employment
(A)	increase	increase	increase
(B)	increase	increase	decrease
(C)	increase	decrease	increase
(D)	decrease	increase	decrease
(E)	decrease	decrease	decrease

32. Which would most likely shift aggregate supply to the right?

(A) An increase in corporate income tax
(B) A decrease in the value of the dollar and an increase in the prices of imported products
(C) An increase in minimum wage
(D) A decrease in business subsidies
(E) Improvements in technology

33. If firms experienced a large and rapid unplanned decrease in inventories, we would anticipate

(A) a reduction in workforce
(B) a decrease in imports
(C) an increase in inflation
(D) a decline in income
(E) a decrease in price levels

34. In the short run, an expansionary fiscal policy will cause aggregate demand, employment, and price level to react in which of the following combinations?

	Aggregate Demand	Employment	Price Level
(A)	decrease	decrease	decrease
(B)	increase	increase	increase
(C)	no change	no change	decrease
(D)	increase	decrease	increase
(E)	decrease	increase	no change

35. If aggregate demand increases and, as a result, the price level increases, while real domestic output and employment are unaffected, we can assume that

    (A) aggregate demand intersects aggregate supply in the intermediate range of the aggregate supply curve
    (B) aggregate demand intersects aggregate supply in the vertical range of the aggregate supply curve
    (C) aggregate demand intersects aggregate supply in the horizontal range of the aggregate supply curve
    (D) aggregate supply increases to accommodate the change in aggregate demand
    (E) aggregate supply has shifted inward due to foreign supply shock

36. The economy experiences an increase in the price level, a decrease in real domestic output, and increased unemployment. Which of the following is the most likely cause?

    (A) Increased productivity
    (B) Increased input prices
    (C) Decreased excess capacity
    (D) Reduced government regulations
    (E) Increased exports

37. Which of the following would a Keynesian recommend to combat high inflation?

    (A) No change in taxation and increased subsidy
    (B) Increased taxation and increased government spending
    (C) Increased taxation and decreased government spending
    (D) Decreased taxation and no change in government spending
    (E) No change in taxation and increased government spending

38. An economy is experiencing hyperinflation. The government wants to reduce household consumption by $48 billion to reduce inflationary pressure. The MPC is 0.75. Which of the following government actions would achieve its objective?

    (A) Increasing spending by $48 billion
    (B) Raising taxes by $6 billion
    (C) Increasing spending by $9 billion and raising taxes by $48 billion
    (D) Raising taxes by $12 billion
    (E) Raising taxes by $16 billion

39. Automatic stabilizers reduce the severity of business cycle fluctuations because they produce changes in the government's budget that

    (A) result in long-run balanced budgets
    (B) result in constant growth of GDP
    (C) help offset changes in employment
    (D) produce a cyclically adjusted budget
    (E) produce a full employment budget

40. One of the criticisms of fiscal policy as a means of regulating the state of the economy is that an "operational lag" occurs between the

    (A) beginning of a recession or inflationary period and the time that it takes for government to become aware of it
    (B) levying of a tax and collection of the revenue
    (C) time the need for fiscal action is recognized and the time that legislation is passed
    (D) time that fiscal action is taken and the time that action has an impact on output, employment, and the price level
    (E) time that taxes have an impact on output, employment, and the price level and the time by which it can be determined if the tax policy is effective

41. The crowding-out effect suggests that

    (A) an increase in household consumption is always at the expense of saving
    (B) any increase in MPC effects a reduction in MPS
    (C) government budget-spending increases close a recessionary gap
    (D) government deficit spending may raise the interest rate and thereby reduce investment
    (E) government borrowing increases the money supply and encourages business investment, thereby reducing household borrowing

42. The United States is experiencing inflation, so Congress adopts a contractionary fiscal policy to reduce inflation. The net export effect suggests that net exports would

(A) decrease due to the resulting decrease in interest rates, thus decreasing aggregate demand and partially reinforcing the fiscal policy
(B) increase, as the decline in the value of the dollar would increase exports
(C) decrease, thus increasing aggregate demand and partially offsetting the fiscal policy
(D) increase, thus decreasing aggregate demand and partially reinforcing the fiscal policy
(E) increase as imports decreased, thus increasing aggregate demand and partially offsetting the fiscal policy

43. A senator calls for legislation reducing corporate taxes, to increase investment and promote economic growth. This senator would most likely be advocating a

(A) contractionary fiscal policy
(B) reduction in automatic stabilizers
(C) nondiscretionary fiscal policy
(D) supply-side fiscal policy
(E) growth in aggregate demand through fiscal policy

44. Other things being equal, the international value of foreign currencies will decrease against the U.S. dollar ($) if

(A) U.S. citizens increase spending on foreign goods
(B) U.S. businesses reduce exports
(C) the U.S. Federal Reserve lowers real interest rates
(D) the number of foreign tourists to Walt Disney World decreases
(E) foreigners increase deposits into U.S. money markets

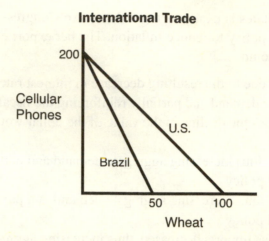

International Trade

45. The domestic opportunity cost of producing 200 cellular phones in the U.S. is 100 bushels of wheat. In Brazil, the domestic opportunity cost of producing 200 cellular phones is 50 bushels of wheat. In this case,

(A) Brazil has a comparative advantage in the production of wheat
(B) One cellular phone costs the United States only 0.25 bushels of wheat
(C) the United States has a comparative advantage in the production of cellular phones
(D) mutual gains from trade can be obtained if the United States imports cellular phones from Brazil and Brazil imports wheat from the United States
(E) mutual gains from trade can be obtained if the United States imports wheat from Brazil and Brazil imports cellular phones from the United States

Nigeria's Production Possibilities						
Commodity Mix	A	B	C	D	E	F
Cocoa	750	600	450	300	150	0
Banana	0	50	100	150	200	250
Colombia's Production Possibilities						
Commodity Mix	A	B	C	D	E	F
Cocoa	2,500	2,000	1,500	1,000	500	0
Banana	0	100	200	300	400	500

46. Based upon the preceding data, the terms of trade will be

   (A) Nigeria wanting at least 2 units of cocoa for 1 unit of banana
   (B) no trade; neither country has a comparative advantage
   (C) more than 4 units of cocoa for 1 unit of banana
   (D) Nigeria wanting more than 5 units of banana for 1 unit of cocoa and Colombia wanting more than 3 units of banana for 1 unit of cocoa
   (E) Nigeria wanting more than 3 units of cocoa for 1 unit of banana and Colombia wanting more than 1 unit of banana for every 5 units of cocoa

47. The U.S. FTC finds Japan guilty of "dumping" steel in the U.S. market. Select the description of a protective tariff response.

   (A) The United States places an excise tax on products that are not produced domestically in order to raise revenues for the steel industry
   (B) The United States places an excise tax on Japanese steel producers, putting them at a competitive disadvantage in selling steel in U.S. domestic markets
   (C) The United States sets a specific maximum amount of steel that may be imported, in a given period of time, to protect U.S. producers of steel
   (D) U.S. steel firms would no longer be allowed to export steel products to Japan
   (E) The United States restricts the issuance of licenses for imported products and sets unreasonable standards for quality or safety in order to restrict imports of steel and protect domestic markets

48. An inflow of investment funds into the United States from overseas is likely to result from

    (A) expectations for reduced U.S. economic growth
    (B) a growing instability in the U.S. dollar value
    (C) a growing belief among investors that the U.S. dollar is overvalued
    (D) a rise in U.S. interest rates relative to world interest rates
    (E) an increase in the U.S. inflation rate

49. The Open Market Committee of the Federal Reserve System (the Fed) is the committee that

    (A) administers FDIC and FSLIC for member banks
    (B) provides advice on banking policy to the Fed
    (C) monitors regulatory banking laws for member banks
    (D) sets policy on the sale and purchase of government bonds by the Fed
    (E) follows the actions and operations of financial markets to keep them open and competitive

50. If bond prices increase, then their

    (A) interest rate will decrease
    (B) interest rate will increase
    (C) transactions demand for money will decrease
    (D) transactions demand for money will increase
    (E) asset demand has decreased

51. A demand deposit at a commercial bank is

    (A) an asset to a bank and a liability to the Fed
    (B) a liability to the depositor and an asset to the bank
    (C) a liability to both the depositor and the bank
    (D) an asset to the depositor and a liability to the bank
    (E) an asset to both the depositor and the bank

52. An individual deposits $10,000 in a commercial bank. The bank is required to hold 20 percent of all deposits on reserve at the regional Federal Reserve Bank. The deposit increases the loan capacity of the bank by

    (A) $11,000
    (B) $10,800
    (C) $9,600
    (D) $8,000
    (E) $6,000

53. If the required reserve ratio is 20 percent, the effective monetary multiplier for the banking system will be

    (A) 2
    (B) 3
    (C) 4
    (D) 5
    (E) 6

54. The primary mission of monetary policy is to assist the economy in achieving

    (A) a rapid pace of economic growth
    (B) an interest rate that constantly supports business investment
    (C) a money supply based on the gold standard
    (D) price stability, economic growth, and full employment level of total output
    (E) a balanced budget consistent with full employment

55. If the Fed buys government bonds from commercial banks in the open market,

    (A) the Fed gives the bonds to the commercial banks, and they pay for them by writing checks that increase their reserves at the Fed
    (B) the banks give the bonds to the Fed, which then increases the reserves of the banks, thereby encouraging higher interest rates
    (C) the Fed gives the bonds to the commercial banks, and they pay for them by writing checks that decrease their reserves at the Fed
    (D) commercial banks give the bonds to the Fed, which then pays for them by increasing the reserves of the commercial banks, thereby encouraging lower interest rates
    (E) commercial banks give the bonds to the Fed, and it pays for them by decreasing the money supply

56. If the Fed sells government bonds to the public in the open market,

(A) the Fed gives the bonds to the public; the public pays for the bonds by writing a check that (when cleared) will increase the money supply

(B) the Fed gives the bonds to the public; the public pays for them by writing checks that (when cleared) will decrease commercial bank reserves at the Fed, raising interest rates

(C) banks buy the bonds from people, increasing the money supply and lowering interest rates

(D) the public gives the bonds to the Fed; the Fed pays for the bonds by check, which (when deposited) decreases the money supply

(E) the public gives the bonds to the Fed; the Fed pays for the bonds by check, which (when deposited) increases interest rates

57. Assume that the required reserve ratio for commercial banks is 20 percent. If the Federal Reserve Banks buy $5 billion in government securities from commercial banks, the lending ability of the banking system will

(A) decrease by $9 billion
(B) increase by $9 billion
(C) increase by $15 billion
(D) increase by $20 billion
(E) increase by $25 billion

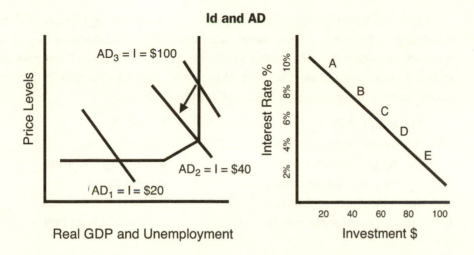

Id and AD

AD$_3$ = I = $100

AD$_2$ = I = $40

AD$_1$ = I = $20

Price Levels

Real GDP and Unemployment

Interest Rate %

10% 8% 6% 4% 2%

A
B
C
D
E

20 40 60 80 100

Investment $

58. Refer to the preceding models, in which the numbers after the AD$_1$, AD$_2$, and AD$_3$ labels indicate the level of investment spending associated with each AD curve. All numbers are in billions of dollars. The interest rate and the level of investment spending in the economy are at point E on the investment demand curve. To achieve noninflationary, full employment output in the economy, the monetary authorities should

(A) decrease AD by increasing the interest rate from 2 to 4 percent
(B) decrease AD by increasing the interest rate from 4 to 6 percent
(C) increase AD by decreasing the interest rate from 4 to 2 percent
(D) increase the level of investment spending from $100 billion to $150 billion
(E) increase interest rates to 8% and reduce AD$_3$ to AD$_2$

59. Which of the following is the most accurate description of events when monetary authorities increase the size of commercial banks' excess reserves?

(A) A fall in interest rates decreases the money supply, causing an increase in investment spending, output, and employment
(B) The money supply is increased, which decreases the interest rate and causes investment spending, output, and employment to increase
(C) A rise in interest rates increases the money supply, causing a decrease in investment spending, output, and employment
(D) The money supply is decreased, which increases the interest rate and causes investment spending, output, and employment to decrease
(E) Bond prices fall, interest rates increase, investment spending rises, and employment and GDP increase

60. Assume that demand-pull inflationary pressure is a growing problem for the economy. In response to this threat, the Federal Reserve decides to pursue a policy to reduce the inflationary pressure. At the same time, Congress decides to eliminate a budget surplus. Which set of policy changes by the Fed and Congress would result, thereby offsetting each other?

Monetary Policy	Fiscal Policy
(A) selling government securities	lowering taxes
(B) buying government securities	increasing spending
(C) selling government bonds	raising taxes
(D) buying government bonds	increasing subsidies
(E) selling government bonds	increasing spending

61. The inflation measurement that would react to a rise in the price of apples, by accounting for the consumer's substitution of oranges, and compare orange prices over the last year would be the

(A) CPI
(B) PCE index
(C) GNP
(D) GDP
(E) real inflation rate

62. A recessionary gap exists when the short-run equilibrium level of real GDP

(A) results in price level rises for two business quarters
(B) equals the NRU
(C) is above the full employment level of real GDP
(D) is below the full employment level of real GDP
(E) is beyond the LRAS

63. The short-run Phillips curve indicates that

    (A) there is a direct relationship between inflation and unemployment.
    (B) there is no trade-off between unemployment and inflation
    (C) as prices rise the quantity demanded decreases
    (D) the natural rate of unemployment is unchanging
    (E) there is an indirect relationship between unemployment and inflation

64. In a six-month period the average price level rose 300%, while John's income rose from $40,000 to $60,000. Which of the following represents the outcome of this monetary event?

	Nominal Income	Real Income
(A)	Increased	Decreased
(B)	Unaffected	Increased
(C)	Increased	Increased
(D)	Decreased	Decreased
(E)	Unaffected	Unaffected

65. If a nation was running a current account surplus with country X, it could prevent its currency from appreciating by

    (A) lowering the price of its goods and services to country X
    (B) encouraging more foreign tourism of country X's residents
    (C) purchasing country X's assets
    (D) selling its foreign assets
    (E) increasing its interest rates

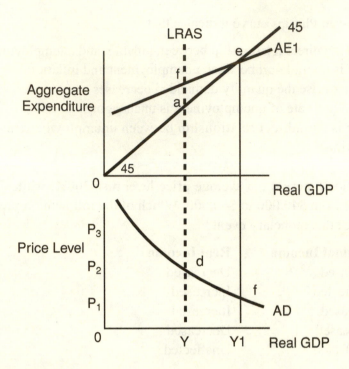

66. What economic problem is depicted in the figure above?

(A) Recessionary gap
(B) Cost-push inflation
(C) High unemployment
(D) Inflationary gap
(E) High interest rates

Use the following graph to answer **Questions 67 and 68**.

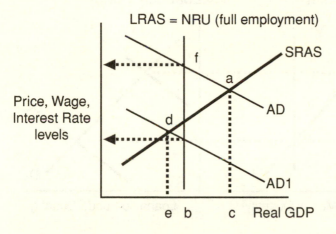

67. In the figure above, equilibrium point a, resulting from SRAS and AD, would be

(A) an economy resulting from economic growth
(B) experiencing deflation
(C) unsustainable in the long run
(D) sustainable in the long run if interest rates were lowered
(E) experiencing unemployment

68. In the figure above, equilibrium point b, resulting from SRAS and AD1, would be

(A) an economy experiencing hyperinflation
(B) an economy experiencing stagflation
(C) an economy with high unemployment
(D) sustainable in the long run
(E) improved if the government raised taxes

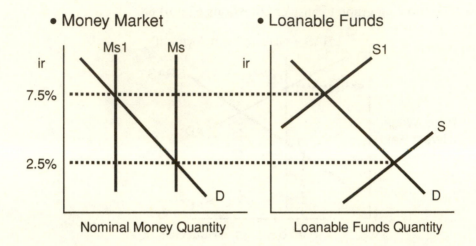

69. The event depicted above illustrates that

    (A) a decrease in the absolute money supply would cause a decrease in the supply of loanable funds
    (B) a tight money supply by the FOMC would not affect loanable funds
    (C) an easy money supply by the FOMC would cause the supply of loanable funds to decrease
    (D) a rate of 7.5% can occur in the money market, and a 2.5% rate can occur in the loanable funds market
    (E) a decrease in the demand for money will occur

70. If domestic real interest rates remain constant at 5.5% and a foreign nation's real interest rates rise to 8.5%, which of the following is the correct domestic reaction?

	Domestic Bonds	Foreign Bonds	Foreign Currency Value
(A)	Prices rise	Sell	Depreciate
(B)	Prices fall	Buy	Appreciate
(C)	Buy	Buy	Unaffected
(D)	Unaffected	Unaffected	Unaffected
(E)	Sell	Buy	Depreciate

71. Assume that a country with an open economy has a fixed exchange rate system and its currency is currently undervalued in the foreign exchange market. Which of the following is true regarding its official exchange rate?

(A) The demand for its currency is insufficient.
(B) The supply curve of the country's currency is horizontal.
(C) The demand curve for the country's currency is horizontal.
(D) The quantity of the country's currency demanded is greater than the quantity supplied.
(E) The quantity of the country's currency supplied is greater than the quantity demanded.

72. If exchange rates are allowed to fluctuate freely and the U.S. demand for Mexican pesos decreased, which of the following will most likely occur?

(A) The dollar price of Mexican goods will decrease.
(B) The peso price of U.S. goods will decrease.
(C) The dollar price of the peso will increase.
(D) The dollar price of Mexican goods will increase.
(E) Importing of Mexican goods will decrease.

73. A surplus in the U.S. current account can be described as an

(A) excess of foreign purchase of U.S. financial assets
(B) event that would deplete U.S. gold reserves
(C) excess of U.S. purchases of foreign financial assets
(D) excess of U.S. purchases of foreign goods and services
(E) excess of foreign purchases of U.S. goods and services

74. If the U.S. balance of payments had a current account surplus, which of the following would also exist?

(A) An equal deficit in the capital account
(B) An equal deficit in the federal budget
(C) An equal surplus in the capital account
(D) A depreciation of the U.S. dollar in the foreign exchange market
(E) A balance in net exports

75. According to the theory of rational expectations, a fully anticipated expansionary fiscal policy causes the price level and real output to react in which of the following combinations?

	Price Level	Real Output
(A)	Increase	Increase
(B)	Increase	Decrease
(C)	No change	No change
(D)	Increase	No change
(E)	No change	Increase

76. Which of the following policies would support increased productivity in a free market economy?

(A) High import quotas
(B) Increased savings rate
(C) Increased taxation
(D) High protective tariffs
(E) Restrictive immigration policies

77. According to a supply-side economist, which of the following statements is true?

(A) A cut in tax rates increases the federal deficit and thus increases aggregate supply.
(B) An increase in the government's supply of transfer payments helps distribute income equitably.
(C) Government should work to balance trade.
(D) An increase in tax rates helps to increase the aggregate demand for goods and stimulate increased aggregate supply.
(E) A cut in tax rates provides increased incentive to invest and produce, thereby shifting the aggregate supply curve to the right.

78. If the national savings rate increased, which of the following shows how real interest rates and investment spending would react?

	Real Interest Rate	Investment Spending
(A)	Increase	Decrease
(B)	No change	Increase
(C)	Decrease	Increase
(D)	Increase	Increase
(E)	Decrease	Decrease

79. According to the short-run Phillips curve, which of the following occurs when the Federal Reserve reduces the money supply?

(A) The unemployment rate and the inflation rate both decrease.
(B) The unemployment rate and the inflation rate both increase.
(C) The inflation rate decreases and the unemployment rate increases.
(D) The inflation rate decreases and the unemployment rate is unchanged.
(E) The inflation rate increases and the unemployment rate decreases.

80. According to monetarist theory, inflation is primarily the result of

(A) an excessive growth in the money supply
(B) excessive investment in capital goods
(C) high federal tax rates
(D) low federal tax rates
(E) too many foreign imported goods

PRACTICE TEST 1

Answer Key

1. (E)	28. (A)	55. (D)
2. (D)	29. (A)	56. (B)
3. (B)	30. (C)	57. (E)
4. (B)	31. (E)	58. (E)
5. (A)	32. (E)	59. (B)
6. (B)	33. (C)	60. (A)
7. (D)	34. (B)	61. (B)
8. (C)	35. (B)	62. (D)
9. (D)	36. (B)	63. (E)
10. (E)	37. (C)	64. (A)
11. (D)	38. (E)	65. (C)
12. (B)	39. (C)	66. (D)
13. (C)	40. (D)	67. (C)
14. (C)	41. (D)	68. (D)
15. (D)	42. (E)	69. (A)
16. (B)	43. (D)	70. (B)
17. (D)	44. (E)	71. (D)
18. (D)	45. (D)	72. (A)
19. (C)	46. (E)	73. (E)
20. (D)	47. (B)	74. (A)
21. (B)	48. (D)	75. (D)
22. (C)	49. (D)	76. (B)
23. (B)	50. (A)	77. (E)
24. (D)	51. (D)	78. (C)
25. (D)	52. (D)	79. (C)
26. (A)	53. (D)	80. (A)
27. (E)	54. (D)	

PRACTICE TEST 1
Detailed Explanations of Answers

1. **(E)**   Answers A through D all involve movements along or a return to the original PPF curve. Remember that if the curve is to shift outward, economic growth must take place. This means that an increase in one or all of the factors of production must occur (increased raw materials, labor, investment goods, or innovation). If cereal making is more efficient, the relationship between inputs of production and the resulting output has improved. You are getting increased cereal production with less input.

2. **(D)**   An economic trade-off occurs when you have two g/s whose inputs are interchangeable and limited. Therefore, there must be a reduction in the output of one g/s (education) in order to increase the output of the alternative g/s (military). A government's resources are limited; it can devote those resources, in various combinations, to construction of military goods or to education goods.

3. **(B)**   Scarcity, by definition, describes the nature of our existence. This simply means that resources are finite when compared to humanity's infinite needs and wants. Scarcity is the driving force behind the creation of all economic systems.

4. **(B)**   Specialization—producing the g/s that you are most efficient in—applies both to the individual and to nations as a whole. Division of labor results in greater overall production, thereby increasing the general wealth. Comparative advantage reveals the economic truth that even though one producer may have superior efficiency when compared to another, both benefit from increased productivity when the less efficient producer focuses on its strength, while the more efficient producer specializes in the alternative good.

5. **(A)**   Comparative advantage demonstrates the efficiency that results from specialization. As individuals or nations specialize, their output relative to their input increases. Therefore, the total combined output for these countries increases. This increase in goods increases the standard of living of both nations.

6. **(B)**   GDP is the total dollar value of all finished goods and services sold in the product market. This is done so that there is no double-counting.

7. **(D)**   The consumer price index (CPI) measures the price change in a fixed basket of goods and services. The prices are compared to those of an established base (index) year; it does not measure from the previous year. This allows more accurate inflation measurement over long periods of time. One of the main criticisms of this tool is that it overestimates inflation, in part because the basket is fixed so that new g/s are excluded and original g/s that may no longer be in demand are retained.

8. **(C)**   In the formula to determine GDP, $C + I_g + G + X_n$, I_g represents the gross investment in capital goods by a firm. Therefore, any expenditure that adds to the future productivity of the firm is classified as an investment. Repurchasing stock in the firm does not alter productivity, so it is not an expenditure on investment.

9. **(D)**   One way to determine GDP is by summing all the expenditures on output. The same data can be compiled by adding all the components of income (in the end, they should be equal). On the expenditure side of GDP, all final goods and services are bought by four sectors. The three domestic sectors are: household consumption (C), business investment (I), and government spending (G). The other component of expenditure is foreign (X) purchase of U.S. g/s minus U.S. purchases of foreign product or exports minus imports (X_n). Therefore, the expenditure formula for determining GDP is $C + I_g + G + X_n$.

10. **(E)**   The expansion phase of the business cycle means, by definition, that the output of the economy (GDP) is increasing. By the very nature of GDP, an increase must mean that employment of inputs is also increasing; as labor is a main input, its employment is also increasing. Since output equals income, if output is increasing then income must also be increasing. Price levels will also begin to rise at some point (stage 2 intermediate). However, if the economy is in deep recession (stage 1 horizontal), output can increase without price rise, as we are using so few inputs that increasing opportunity costs have not begun to have an effect on cost and thus price.

11. **(D)**   A decrease in aggregate demand results in a change in aggregate supply quantity. If consumption of autos declines, then the quantity of steel supplied, as an intermediate good, would also decline. If output declines, then jobs and income must also decline.

12. **(B)**   Structural unemployment, by definition, is the result of a mismatch of skills or location. This is a mismatch of job skills, as the robot has replaced the worker.

13. **(C)**   Full employment does not mean 100% employment. By the very definition of structural and frictional unemployment, there will always be unemployed people. Therefore, to determine the unemployment due to a downturn in the business cycle, it is necessary to discount the structurally and frictionally unemployed.

14. **(C)** The second stage of the AS curve, as one moves rightward, represents diminishing marginal productivity and increasing opportunity costs that lead to rising price levels. If we reduce the aggregate demand, the AD curve moves inward, resulting in lower output, employment, and disposable income. These changes would result in overall lower price levels. Also, as fewer resource inputs are required by producers, marginal productivity would actually increase, cost per unit would decline, and a lower price would be charged.

15. **(D)** The vertical stage three of AS represents an economy that has reached maximum productivity. All resource inputs are being used. Therefore, any increase in aggregate demand cannot be met with increased production. Because demand has increased while supply has remained fixed, a higher price level results. This is sometimes referred to as "hyperinflation," as the rise in prices in this environment can be very large.

AD/AS

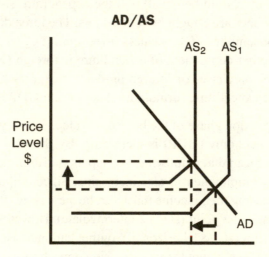

GDP, Income, and Employment

16. **(B)** Transportation input is a variable cost of supply. As more transportation is used, the cost per unit produced increases. An increase in marginal costs would be represented by a shift inward and upward of the AS curve as MC equals the supply curve. In the short run AD would remain fixed, so the result would be a decrease in output (GDP) and a rise in prices.

17. **(D)** Keynes challenged the long-held assumption of Classical economists that long-run AS is perfectly inelastic. They reasoned that price levels, output, and employment were self-regulating. Keynes argued that an economy can become fixed in a cycle of long-run recession, from which it will recover only if stimulated. Keynes argued that by increasing spending and cutting taxes (budget deficit) to the household, the C element of aggregate expenditure will stimulate expansion in the economy.

18. **(D)** By definition, the factor market is where firms purchase the inputs of production. In a free market, individual households own the input factors. Firms pay input owners, which is the household income. The product market, by definition, is where firms sell the finished product to individual households. The product market is the revenue source for firms, and households expend their income in consuming those g/s.

19. **(C)** Income has a direct relationship to aggregate expenditure. If disposable income increases, then expenditure also increases in relation to the MPC.

Aggregate Expenditure and Disposable Income

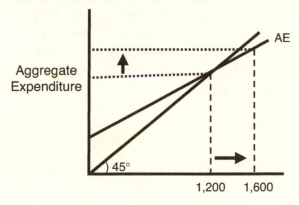

20. **(D)** Bonds are an investment alternative to holding cash. Remember that inflation erodes the value of currency over time. Bonds (corporate and government) are promissory notes whereby the buyer loans money to the seller in exchange for repayment of the loaned amount (principal) plus a set interest rate of return at a set date of maturity. The risk in this investment is that the buyer foregoes the current purchasing power of the currency, in the belief that the interest payment will more than cover any inflation that might occur over the length of the bond maturity—hence, the speculatory nature of the investment.

21. **(B)** When interest rates fall (8% to 2%) and business expectations change, a shift in investment demand (Id to Id_1) will stimulate an increase in the I_g component of AE (AE to AE_1).

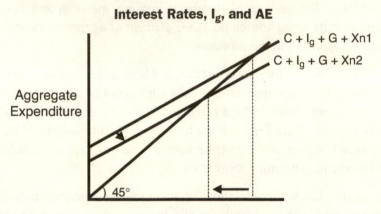

Interest Rates, I_g, and AE

Aggregate Expenditure

$C + I_g + G + Xn1$

$C + I_g + G + Xn2$

45°

GDP, Employment, and Disposable Income

22. **(C)** A change in AE of $25 billion results in an increase in output of $100 billion. [Give the necessary data to determine the MPC/MPS and the multiplier]. Since an AE change of 25 yields a 100 change in output, the multiplier is 4 (25 × 4 = 100). To have a multiplier of 4, the MPS must be 0.25 and the MPC 0.75. This is so because 1/MPS (1/0.25 = 4) = the multiplier and 1 – MPS (1 – 0.25 = 0.75) = MPC.

23. **(B)** Exports, as a component of AE, are an injection into the economy. If exports fell and all else remained equal, the AE would decrease and the equilibrium level of GDP would decrease.

Interest Rates, I_g, and AE

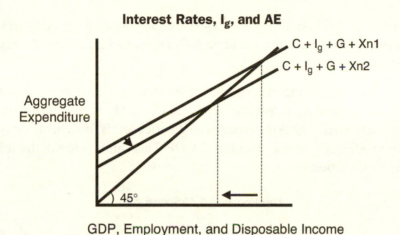

GDP, Employment, and Disposable Income

24. **(D)** The injection-leakage analysis of AE/GDP considers, by definition, leakages to consist of savings, taxes, and imports. All three items represent no spending in the domestic economy.

25. **(D)** [This question tests knowledge of the unique relationship of tax, consumer behavior, and change in AE.] Consumers will react to taxes by adjusting their savings in an amount determined by their MPS. Tax increases will be offset by a reduction in savings. In this case, a $40 billion dollar tax levy would be compensated for, by consumers, through a reduction in savings of $10 billion ($40 \times 0.25 = 10$).

26. **(A)** [This question follows up the concept discussed in question 25.] The reaction of consumers to a tax increase, which is then subject to the multiplier, explains what is known as the balanced budget multiplier. This gap is always equal to a factor of 1. In other words, any equal combination of spending increase and tax increase ($100 million spending and $100 million tax increase adds $100 million to the GDP), will always result in that amount added to the economy. This is because government spending is subject to the full multiplier, whereas taxes are first reduced by the MPS and then subject to the multiplier. Thus, a recessionary or inflationary gap always results from equal amounts of spending and tax quantities.

27. **(E)** The multiplier is 4. The formula to determine the multiplier is:

$$\frac{\text{change in real GDP}}{\text{change in real spending}}, \text{so} \ \frac{1,600 - 1,200}{400 - 300} = \frac{400}{100} = 4$$

28. **(A)** $1,200 billion. If this is a closed economy without a government sector, the aggregate expenditure would be 300 and the multiplier would remain at 4; $300 \times 4 = 1,200$.

29. **(A)** Purchase of imports is a leakage from domestic aggregate expenditure, so it would cause X_n to decrease. If AE falls from AE_1 to AE_2, then so does AD, from AD_1 to AD_2. As AD decreases so do price levels (depending on relationship to AS stage), employment, and GDP. This can be seen in the following graphic depiction:

Decline in AD/AS and AE

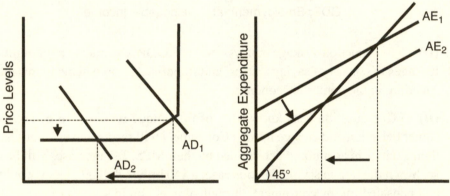

Real GDP and Unemployment   GDP, Employment, and Income

30. **(C)** An increase in the money supply would put more income into the aggregate expenditure. This in turn would increase the aggregate demand. A decrease in interest rates would also help to stimulate aggregate demand, as lower rates encourage borrowing and spending. Both activities stimulate an economy.

31. **(E)** Business investment is a component of AE and thus has a direct influence on AD. If the other three elements of AE remained constant and I_g decreased, then AE would move downward and the AD would move inward. This is depicted in the two models above. Notice that price levels, GDP, and employment all decrease.

32. **(E)** Technology affects productivity. A technical improvement would by definition increase productivity, thereby lowering costs. A lowering of costs and increased productivity shifts the AS curve outward. This outward shift serves to decrease prices, increase output, increase income, and create employment. This could be summed up as an increase in the overall standard of living. The following model shows this event graphically:

Increase in AS

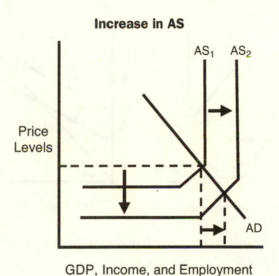

GDP, Income, and Employment

33. **(C)** If firms experienced an unplanned and rapid decrease in inventories, this means that AD has shifted to the right. A large increase in the money supply occurred and there are few additional g/s with which to immediately replace depleted inventories. When money enters the economy while few g/s enter, inflation is by definition a result. Also notice that in the AD/AS model, as you enter stages 2 and 3, price levels rise.

34. **(B)** In the short run, supply is fixed. If government increases spending while at the same time cutting taxes, the AE will increase, causing the AD to increase (move to the right). This change in AD causes an increase in employment and an increase in price levels.

Increase in AD/AS and AE

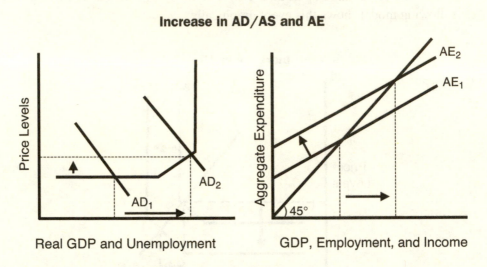

Real GDP and Unemployment   GDP, Employment, and Income

35. **(B)** If AD increases and as a result price levels rise, while GDP and employment are unaffected, the AD must be in stage 3 of the AS. This results in hyperinflation. Notice the extreme rise in prices that results from these events.

AD/AS Hyperinflation

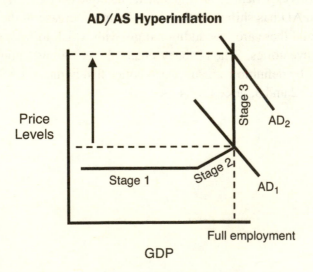

36. **(B)** For that combination to occur in the economy, the AS must have moved inward. When there is a supply shock, there is an unexpected increase in input prices, price levels rise, and GDP and employment decline.

Decrease in AS

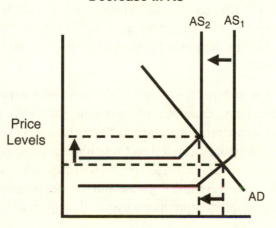

Output, Income, and Employment

37. **(C)** Keynes advocated government intervention in the business cycle to manage the economy in an attempt to moderate the extremes of the business cycle. Through fiscal policy, the government can counter the cycle, stimulating during recession and contracting during expansion. So, if inflation were occurring because of an AD that is too high, the government could cause a contraction in the consumption segment of AD by increasing taxes and reducing government spending.

Decrease in Aggregate Expenditure

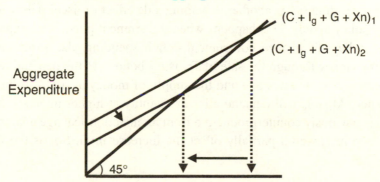

GDP, Employment, and Disposable Income

38. **(E)** [The basis for this answer involves a knowledge of both the multiplier and the realization that a change in tax is partially absorbed by the marginal propensity to save (prior to the effect of the multiplier).] With an MPC of 0.75, the MPS is 0.25; therefore, the initial tax change must be reduced by 0.25. A tax raise of *$16 billion* would first be offset by a $4 billion reduction in household savings. The remainder of $12 billion (16 – 4 = 12) is then subject to the multiplier, which is 4 because it equals 1/MPS (1/0.25 = 4). A $12 billion net tax would reduce the household consumption component of GDP by $48 billion (12 × 4 = 48).

39. **(C)** Automatic stabilizers increase or decrease with expansion and contraction of the economy. Examples of automatic stabilizers are unemployment insurance and Temporary Assistance to Needy Families (TANF). Tax revenues also change automatically, in a direct relationship with the business cycle. If GDP rises, tax revenues increase and transfer payments decline. Conversely, as GDP declines, tax revenues decrease and transfer payments increase. Therefore, automatic stabilizers produce a cyclically adjusted budget.

40. **(D)** There are many criticisms of fiscal policy. The main one is the time lags that occur in the recognition, construction, and operational impact of that policy on the business cycle. Another is that the degree of economic influence desired (great or small stimulus/contraction) is difficult to judge (fiscal policy can be like trying to swat a mosquito with a sledge hammer). Many times fiscal policy of an expansionary nature begins to have an impact long after the recession has passed. This is the advantage that monetary policy enjoys over fiscal policy, both in the almost immediate impact and the degree of influence desired. However, neo-classical economists do contend that both monetary and fiscal stimulus/contraction power may be necessary to manage the state of the economy.

41. **(D)** Crowding out is another damaging side effect of fiscal policy that monetary policy avoids. This happens when government pursues an expansionary fiscal policy. To finance government deficit spending, the government must borrow money through the sale of Treasury bonds. As the demand for money increases, interest rates rise and the supply of money available to business is lessened. Also, I_g will demand a lower quantity at higher interest-rate prices. This is obviously counterproductive from an injection-leakage analysis, as the decrease in I_g would partially offset the increase in G. So, as the following

diagram shows, interest rates would rise from 4% to 8%, reducing the I_g component of AE. The AD/AS model demonstrates the intended results of fiscal policy, moving AD_1 to AD_2 with the actual lessened impact AD_1 to AD_{2a}, due to crowding out. Most economists contend, however, that this crowding-out effect would be rendered irrelevant during recession if the Federal Reserve cooperated with an easing of money policy.

Crowding Out

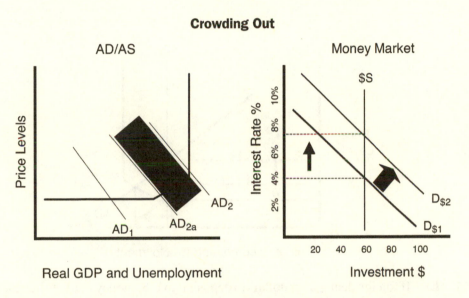

42. **(E)** When Congress pursues a contractionary fiscal policy, it reduces spending and increases taxes. The result of this behavior is to decrease the money supply. This causes interest rates to rise, discouraging households from purchasing g/s (both domestic and foreign). Initially, the weak dollar (due to inflation) coupled with stronger foreign currencies results in exports rising while imports fall. Thus, the X_n component of AE/AD increases and partially offsets the decrease in the C, I_g, and G components. In the long run, the higher interest rates attract foreign investors and the increased demand for the dollar causes it to appreciate, reversing the trade balance trend (long-run trade equilibrium concept).

43. **(D)** Supply-side economists contend that tax reductions aimed at the I_g will promote increases in productivity and thus output, along with job creation and higher income. This is attained without inflation because the increase

in income is equal to the increase in output. This is a revisit of Say's Law. Many economists are critical of the degree to which tax cuts affect investment and thus AS expansion. Some contend that the lower tax rates only serve to enhance the wealth of business owners and further distort income distribution. This area continues to be investigated by economists for evidence of some impact of tax policy on AS expansion.

Increase in AS

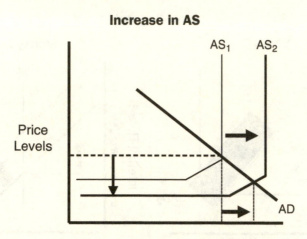

Output, Income, and Employment

44. **(E)** If foreign demand for dollars to deposit into U.S. money markets increases (D_1 to D_2), then the value of the dollar will appreciate, because the foreign currencies would depreciate (5 to 7.5 foreign currency units per dollar).

The Currency Money Market

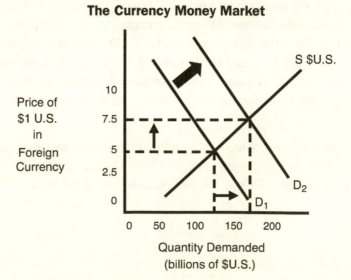

Quantity Demanded
(billions of $U.S.)

45. **(D)**   [This answer is based on the principle of comparative advantage.] Total output for two nations will be greatest when each good is produced by the one that has the lower domestic opportunity cost for that good. This is determined by calculating the ratio of the domestic opportunity cost. In the case of Brazil and the United States, the United States must give up 100 units of wheat to get 200 cellular phones (2cp = 1w). For Brazil, 50 units of wheat must be sacrificed to gain 200 phones (2cp = 0.5w). Brazil has the lower cost of producing cell phones, since 1cp = 0.25 w and for the United States 1cp = 0.5 w. Both benefit by Brazil producing phones and the United States producing wheat and then trading. Both gain from specializing. If we assume that both nations were separately producing at the midpoint of their production possibilities, they would create the following scenario. They have 25 more units of wheat than before specialization.

Country	Before Specialization	After Specialization	Net Change	Gains from Trade
United States	100 cell phones 50 wheat	0 cell phones 100 wheat	–100 cell phones + 50 wheat	0 cell phone + 25 wheat
Brazil	100 cell phones 25 wheat	200 cell phones 0 wheat	+100 cell phones – 25 wheat	

46. **(E)**   [This answer is based on comparative advantage analysis, as shown in the answer to question 45, and adding the terms of trade principle.] After specialization, countries will want more goods than they had prior to it. They must receive a ratio of return greater than they had from their domestic production. In this case, Nigeria (3 cocoa for 1 banana) produces bananas and Colombia (5 cocoa for 1 banana) produces cocoa. Nigeria will want to get more than its domestic return of 3 cocoa for 1 banana (say, 4 cocoa for 1 banana +1), which increases its standard of living. Colombia will want to get a greater return than its domestic production of 1 banana for 5 cocoa (say, 1.25 banana for 5 cocoa).

47. **(B)**   "Dumping" is when a nation (or firm) sells a good below cost as a means of harming its competition. Under the rules established by the WTO, countries found guilty of dumping goods in another nation's market may be penalized by the WTO, which may allow the offended nation to place a tariff on the foreign producer's good as a remedy. This tax punishes the offending nation and returns the field to a competitive market.

48. **(D)** If interest rates rose in the United States, the higher rate of return on invested money would attract foreign investors. Because they have to exchange their foreign currency into dollars to purchase U.S. securities, the demand for U.S. dollars would increase. If the demand for dollars increased, the value of the dollar would appreciate (see model for question 44).

49. **(D)** The FOMC is the monetary policy-making branch of the Federal Reserve System. Its membership of five Fed bank presidents and the seven members of the Board of Governors meets approximately every six weeks to set the discount rate and the federal funds rate. The federal funds rate is attained through the sale or purchase of Treasury bonds in the open market.

50. **(A)** Critical to FOMC policy is the indirect relationship that exists between bond prices and their interest yield. When bond prices rise (say, due to increased demand), the interest rate yield on those bonds declines. If the FOMC increases the money supply by purchasing bonds, their yield would decline (as would interest rates—easy money). If the Fed decreases the money supply by selling bonds, their yield would increase (as would interest rates—tight money).

51. **(D)** By definition, a deposit at a bank is placed on the bank's books as a liability, as this is money that is owed by the bank to the depositor. The deposit is an asset to the depositor, as it represents value owned by the depositor.

52. **(D)** This function is at the heart of the fractional reserve banking system. The Federal Reserve sets a reserve ratio requirement for member banks. Reserves in excess of this required amount are available for loan. In this case, the reserve is 20%; if $10,000 is deposited, then $2,000 is reserved with the Fed and $8,000 is available to loan.

53. **(D)** Because loan proceeds are deposited by the recipients into their banks, that action adds to the reserves of that depository. The additional deposit, after the reserve ratio is met, increases the depository's assets and the money is re-loaned. This is known as the money multiplier. The formula is 1/reserve ratio requirement. In this case, the rrr is 0.20, so the multiplier is 5 ($1/0.20 = 5$).

54. **(D)** The established mission of the Federal Reserve and its monetary policy is to achieve price stability, an environment conducive to economic growth, and full employment.

55. **(D)** When the FOMC orders bonds to be purchased from commercial banks, the bond is given to the Fed in exchange for a credit to the reserves of the commercial bank. This credit enables the bank to increase its loans and thus the money supply. This increase in the money supply relative to the demand for money generally lowers interest rates, thereby encouraging expansion in the economy.

56. **(B)** This action has the opposite impact of the action taken in question 55. When the Fed sells bonds, it removes money from circulation and replaces it with a bond. As money is removed from the market, available interest rates rise. Also, as the supply of bonds in the bond market increases, their price decreases. As mentioned earlier, this increases their interest rate yield.

57. **(E)** If the reserve is 20 percent, the multiplier is 5 ($1/0.20 = 5$). If $5 billion is added to commercial bank reserves, 5 times that amount would eventually enter the economy ($5 billion $\times$ 5 = 25$).

58. **(E)** The current interest rates are too expansionary and as a result the economy is in hyperinflation. From the money market model, it is clear that at $I = $40 billion$, the interest rate is 8%. The higher interest rate would tighten money, slow expenditure, and move AD back to stage 2.

Id and AD/AS

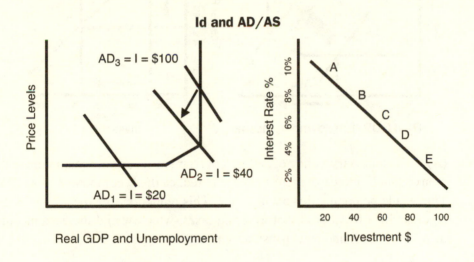

Real GDP and Unemployment

Investment $

59. **(B)** [This question again focuses on the relationship between interest rates, I_g, AE, AD, and GDP.] In this case, monetary policy has been one of easy money ($S1 to $S2) that encourages (interest rates 10% to 4%) business investment ($20 to $80), thus increasing the AE/AD (AD_1 to AD_2) and stimulating expansion of the economy. When output increases, so too do employment and income.

Fed "Easy Money" Policy
The Money Market and AD/AS

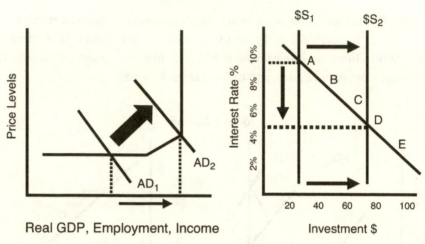

60. **(A)** The monetary policy of selling government securities would reduce the money supply, increase interest rates, and reduce the I_g component of AE/AD. This would be contractionary in nature. This reduction of expenditure would be offset by a fiscal policy of lowering taxes, which would increase income, increase AE/AD, and be expansionary in nature.

61. **(B)** The PCE index measures actual consumption. This allows for consumer substitutions if the price of a good rises. The PCE then links that good to its prior year's price, giving a better short-run inflation indicator.

62. **(D)** A recessionary gap occurs when the aggregate demand intersects the SRAS below the full employment level. This indicates that unemployed resource inputs exist and the economy is operating below potential.

63. **(E)** The short-run Phillips curve can operate inside or outside the natural rate of unemployment. If inside the NRU (LRAS), the increased unemployment drives wages and prices down. In the long run, however, the indirect relationship between unemployment and inflation will lower prices and stimulate an increase in AD returning to the NRU (LRAS) level. Beyond the NRU, the opposite would occur.

64. **(A)** Nominal income increased by 50%, but because of the 300% rise in prices, real wages, or purchasing power, would actually be eroded by 250%.

65. **(C)** The balance of payments is the current account plus the financial account. If a current account deficit was offset by an equal financial account surplus (foreign purchase of domestic assets), currency values would not change because the supply and demand of currencies would be constant.

66. **(D)** An inflationary gap occurs when the aggregate expenditure exceeds the full employment level of an economy to provide the output demanded. As this occurs, prices rise but output does not, and inflation of a demand-pull results.

67. **(C)** This point is unsustainable because an economy cannot operate outside its PPF curve, which is determined by its resource limits.

68. **(D)** This point is sustainable because an economy can operate indefinitely inside its full potential. The result is inefficient employment of resources and a lower standard of living.

69. **(A)** In time the loanable funds market would see a decrease in the supply of funds by lenders. In reaction to a decrease in the absolute money supply, real GDP would decline, incomes would fall, and savings would decrease.

70. **(B)** Investors are attracted to profit and repelled by loss. Therefore, domestic bondholders would sell their bonds (causing prices to fall) and buy the foreign bonds as they receive a higher yield. Because foreign bonds must be purchased with foreign currency, the demand for foreign currency would increase and the price of the foreign currency would rise (appreciation).

71. **(D)** A fixed exchange rate means that a government's central bank has a set or pegged exchange rate (i.e., 100 yen = 1 dollar). If Americans' demand for Japanese goods increased, more yen would be demanded. Because the quantity supplied is unchanged, a shortage of yen would occur in the currency market, thereby appreciating the value of the yen. (Because it would take more dollars to buy a yen, prices of Japanese exports would rise.)

However, since the foreign nation has a set rate, the dilemma for the Japanese central bank is that it must either increase the supply of yen (inflationary in Japan) or purchase and hold American dollars in its excess foreign reserves. Rather than hold U.S. dollars, an alternative solution would be to buy U.S. financial assets, such as government bonds (a process also known as currency sterilization).

This short-run solution (which keeps the import price of Japanese goods constant while export sales continue and jobs are unchanged) prevents trade equilibrium from occurring. In the long run, if left uncorrected, this behavior could lead to a serious "bubble" of currency inequality that when burst would result in serious damage to both economies. The result would be significant inflation, unemployment, and lowered standards of living.

72. **(A)**   When the domestic demand for a foreign currency decreases, its price in the foreign currency falls. This depreciation of value means that the price of the foreign currency requires fewer domestic dollars, making it cheaper.

73. **(E)**   The current account measures net exports of goods and services. A surplus in the current account indicates that foreign nations are buying more U.S. goods and services than the United States is buying of theirs.

74. **(A)**   Because a balance of payments must equal an accounting zero, any surplus in the current account either must be reflected as a decrease in the excess reserve of foreign money or, if used to buy foreign assets, must appear as a deficit in the capital account.

75. **(D)**   Rational expectations is a key element of neoclassical economic theory (see definition in the Glossary). For example, when the federal government deficit spends, producers realize that this is an inflationary action and respond by raising prices to offset the reduced dollar value. Producers do not change output because higher prices would forestall any increase in aggregate demand.

76. **(B)**   Because savings must equal investment (S = Ig), an increase in the savings rate allows an economy (with a larger capital pool from which to borrow) to increase its investment in capital goods. Growth of capital goods allows for increased output through productivity growth.

77. **(E)**   Supply-side economic theory stems in part from Say's Law (supply creates its own demand) and the Laffer curve (tax cuts increase tax revenues; as the economy grows, a greater national income is taxable). When taxes are cut, investors keep a larger share of the profits. This stimulates investment in capital goods, which creates jobs (real output equals real income), increased output (the AS curve shifts to the right), and increased demand.

78. **(C)**   When the savings rate increases, the money supply available for banks to lend increases. An increase in the supply of money to lend lowers the price of money (real interest rates), and as the price falls, the quantity demanded by investors increases.

79. **(C)**   In the short-run Phillips curve, an inverse relationship exists between inflation and unemployment. A reduction of the money supply (the Federal Reserve sells bonds) causes a rise in nominal interest rates (money is withdrawn from banks because higher returns are available in the bond market).

As real interest rates rise (the bank's money supply decreases) in reaction to the Fed's actions, the quantity demanded by investors decreases. As aggregate demand decreases, price levels fall (disinflation or even deflation). As aggregate demand falls, the quantity supplied falls. Thus, layoffs occur.

80. **(A)**   As Milton Friedman said, "Inflation is always a monetary event." In other words, inflation is simply too much money chasing too few goods. Thus, the two main causes of inflation are either demand-pull or cost-push. In either case, the relationship between the goods and the money supply changes, resulting in a money supply increase relative to the supply of goods. Many economists have stated that, historically, poor fiscal policy (deficit spending) is the main cause of inflation.

PRACTICE TEST 2

CLEP Macroeconomics

Also available at the REA Study Center (*www.rea.com/studycenter*)

This practice test is also offered online at the REA Study Center. Since all CLEP exams are administered on computer, we recommend that you take the online version of the test to receive these added benefits:

- **Timed testing conditions** – Gauge how much time you can spend on each question.
- **Automatic scoring** – Find out how you did on the test, instantly.
- **On-screen detailed explanations of answers** – Learn not just the correct answer, but also why the other answer choices are incorrect.
- **Diagnostic score reports** – Pinpoint where you're strongest and where you need to focus your study.

PRACTICE TEST 2

CLEP Macroeconomics

(Answer sheets appear in the back of the book.)

TIME: 90 Minutes
80 Questions

DIRECTIONS: Each of the questions or incomplete statements below is followed by five possible answers or completions. Select the best choice in each case and fill in the corresponding oval on the answer sheet.

1. The fundamental problem associated with economics is

    (A) establishing a government agency responsible for the management of goods and services
    (B) the scarcity of productive resources compared with societal wants
    (C) arriving at an acceptable distribution of goods and services
    (D) determining the equilibrium level of output
    (E) determining the allocative and productive efficiency levels of output

2. The payments of money associated with the four resource inputs of land, labor, capital, and entrepreneurial efforts are, respectively,

    (A) rent, wage, interest, and profit/loss
    (B) wage, rent, interest, and profit/loss
    (C) interest, profit/loss, rent, and wage
    (D) profit/loss, rent, wage, and interest
    (E) there are no money payments in the resource market

3. In a free-market economy, *productive efficiency* means

    (A) the mix of goods and services that society deems appropriate
    (B) making the most goods and services possible
    (C) employing every citizen in the production process
    (D) producing within the limits of the production possibility frontier curve
    (E) that the society is employing the least-cost method of production

4. Trade-offs are unequal and the production possibility frontier (PPF) curve bows outward because of the

   (A) scarcity of resources
   (B) unequal prices of the four factors of production
   (C) productive inequality of resource inputs in producing every good or service
   (D) productive equality of resource inputs in producing every good or service
   (E) allocative inefficiency of society

5. When trying to decide whether to go to a movie or study for a CLEP exam, you are confronted with

   (A) money and interest issues
   (B) economic choice and opportunity cost
   (C) the law of supply and demand
   (D) socioeconomic goals
   (E) scarcity and derived demand

6. The marginal cost curve is

   (A) downward sloping because of diminishing marginal utility
   (B) upward sloping because of diminishing marginal utility
   (C) downward sloping because of increasing marginal returns
   (D) upward sloping because of increasing opportunity costs
   (E) perfectly elastic when the good has a substitute

7. Country Xeta has a consumer price index of 110 in year 1 and 120 in year 2. How much inflation did Xeta experience, if any?

   (A) 10%
   (B) 20%
   (C) Deflation rather than inflation took place
   (D) 0.10%
   (E) 9%

8. Assume that an economy is producing at an output that places it on its PPF curve. Then the labor force increases yet no new jobs are created. How are economists likely to view these events?

   (A) The production possibilities increased.
   (B) The production possibilities did not change but are operating inside the curve.
   (C) Movement along the curve has occurred.
   (D) The PPF shifted inward, but the economy is now producing outside the curve.
   (E) The PPF shifted outward, but the economy is now producing inside the curve.

9. Most free-market banking systems are based on

   (A) money with intrinsic value
   (B) fractional reserves
   (C) commodities
   (D) hard currency
   (E) gold reserves

10. The demand curve is downward sloping

    (A) because of the law of diminishing returns
    (B) because tastes and preferences often change
    (C) to represent the consumption loss resulting from decreased consumer income
    (D) because of diminishing marginal utility
    (E) because to sell their goods when costs rise, producers have to lower their prices

11. A person who is seeking a job but does not have the skills necessary to qualify for any of the available jobs is considered

    (A) structurally unemployed
    (B) frictionally unemployed
    (C) cyclically unemployed
    (D) seasonally unemployed
    (E) not part of the labor force

12. Which of the following incurs the greatest harm from unexpected inflation?

    (A) Government
    (B) Borrowers
    (C) Debtors
    (D) Lenders
    (E) Income earners

13. Select the untrue statement regarding the concept of a natural rate of unemployment.

    (A) It is a constant rate of 4.5%.
    (B) It is the rate that, if exceeded by aggregate demand, leads to inflation.
    (C) It is not a constant rate that economists can agree on.
    (D) It is the rate at which no cyclical employment exists.
    (E) It is the rate at which frictional unemployment exists.

14. In an open economy, when consumption increases, gross domestic product (GDP) is expected to

    (A) increase
    (B) decrease
    (C) remain constant
    (D) see wage inflation
    (E) be affected in an unpredictable manner

15. The annual GDP of a country is a measure of the final retail sales dollar value of all the goods and services

    (A) consumed by that country in a year
    (B) manufactured by that country in a year
    (C) produced by that country in a year, excluding exports
    (D) produced by that country in a year, excluding imports
    (E) produced by that country in a year

16. Which of the following events would increase employment and lower the price level in the United States?

    (A) Increase in consumption
    (B) Increase in productivity
    (C) Decrease in the population
    (D) Increase in exports
    (E) Increase in the wage rate

17. What is likely to happen to nominal interest rates, investment, and aggregate demand if the Federal Open Market Committee (FOMC) orders the sale of bonds?

	Interest Rates	Investment	Aggregate Demand
(A)	Increase	Increase	Increase
(B)	Decrease	Decrease	Decrease
(C)	Increase	Increase	Decrease
(D)	Increase	Decrease	Decrease
(E)	Decrease	Increase	Increase

18. If the marginal propensity to save (MPS) is 40%, what is the simple spending multiplier?

(A) 1.25
(B) 2.5
(C) 4
(D) 5
(E) 8

19. When do government deficits lead to the crowding-out effect?

(A) When government deficit spending forces private investment to contract
(B) When government deficit spending causes an increase in real GDP, which leads to a decrease in private investment
(C) When government deficit spending leads to a decrease in real GDP, which leads to a drop in real interest rates
(D) When government deficit spending leads to a decrease in foreign capital flows into the country.
(E) When government deficit spending is not accompanied by the purchase of government bonds by the Federal Reserve

20. If the international value of a country's currency depreciates, what is the most likely impact on its short-run aggregate supply and demand?

    (A) Short-run aggregate supply shifts to the right, and aggregate demand shifts to the right.
    (B) Short-run aggregate supply shifts to the left, and aggregate demand shifts to the left.
    (C) Short-run aggregate supply shifts to the right, and aggregate demand shifts to the left.
    (D) Short-run aggregate supply shifts to the left, and aggregate demand shifts to the right.
    (E) Short-run aggregate supply shifts to the right, and aggregate demand remains constant.

21. If the international value of a country's currency appreciates, what is the most likely impact on its exports?

    (A) Increase
    (B) Decrease
    (C) No effect
    (D) Increase goods, decrease services
    (E) Decrease goods, increase services

22. Select the item that would be included in GDP.

    (A) Bronze used in the manufacture of a faucet
    (B) Corn seeds planted by a farmer
    (C) Windshield wipers purchased by Ford Motor Company
    (D) An illegal football bet placed by an economics teacher
    (E) Payment to a barber for a haircut

23. The difference between nominal and real GDP is that real GDP

    (A) excludes Social Security
    (B) includes production by U.S. companies overseas
    (C) is adjusted by a price index
    (D) adjusts for resource import price levels
    (E) includes all transfer payments

24. An increase in the money supply is most likely to have which of the following short-run effects on real interest rates and real output?

	Real Interest Rates	Real Output
(A)	Decrease	Decrease
(B)	Decrease	Increase
(C)	Increase	Decrease
(D)	Increase	No change
(E)	No change	Increase

Use the following economic model to answer **Questions 25 and 26**.

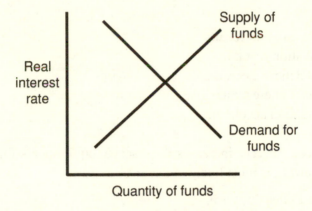

25. Assume that a perfectly competitive financial market exists. If the government increases its deficit spending, what effect does that have on the real interest rate and long-run economic growth?

	Real Interest Rate	Long-Run Economic Growth
(A)	Increase	Increase
(B)	Decrease	Decrease
(C)	Decrease	Increase
(D)	Increase	No change
(E)	Increase	Decrease

26. Identify the impact that the event depicted in the model has on net exports and capital inflow.

	Net Exports	**Capital Inflow**
(A)	Increase	Decrease
(B)	Increase	No change
(C)	Decrease	Increase
(D)	Decrease	No change
(E)	No change	No change

27. If an economy is operating at a fully-employed capacity, what is the impact of a large increase in the money supply, based on the quantity theory of money?

    (A) Severe inflation results
    (B) Disinflation results
    (C) Fiscal deficits decrease
    (D) Nominal interest rates rise
    (E) Job creation accelerates

28. If the Federal Reserve increases the reserve requirements for banks, which of the following is most likely to occur?

    (A) Interest rates decrease.
    (B) Exports decrease.
    (C) The international value of the nation's currency depreciates.
    (D) Investments increase.
    (E) Financial capital flows out of the country.

29. If the Federal Reserve increases the federal funds rate for banks, which of the following is most likely to occur?

    (A) Interest rates decrease.
    (B) Exports decrease.
    (C) The international value of the nation's currency depreciates.
    (D) Investments increase.
    (E) Financial capital flows out of the country.

30. A typical U.S. consumer budget, which included the following purchases in 2004 to 2005, is shown below.

Item	Quantity	2004 Price	2005 Price
Bread	5	$5.00	$6.00
Butter	1	$2.00	$3.00
Jam	1	$3.00	$7.00

What conclusion can you make regarding the rate of inflation?

(A) Inflation was 40%.
(B) Deflation was present in bread.
(C) Inflation increased by 10%.
(D) Inflation increased by 60%.
(E) Inflation increased by 33%.

31. If the Federal Reserve decreases the federal funds rate for banks, which of the following is least likely to occur?

(A) Interest rates decrease.
(B) Exports decrease.
(C) The international value of the nation's currency depreciates.
(D) Investments increase.
(E) Financial capital flows out of the country.

32. If the nominal GDP is $400 billion and the GDP deflator is 0.8, then the real GDP is

(A) $80 billion
(B) $92 billion
(C) $250 billion
(D) $320 billion
(E) $12.5 billion

33. If government purchases increase $10 billion and the MPC is 0.75, what is the final effect on the economy?

(A) The marginal propensity to consume is less than 1.
(B) The GDP increases by $40 billion.
(C) The GDP increases by $17.5 billion.
(D) The MPS increases.
(E) The GDP increases by $7.5 billion.

34. What happens in the short run when fiscal policy makers decide to increase government spending by $200 billion but balance the budget by raising taxes by an equal amount of $200 billion?

    (A) The aggregate demand does not change.
    (B) The aggregate demand shifts to the left.
    (C) The aggregate demand shifts to the right.
    (D) The short-run aggregate supply shifts to the left.
    (E) The short-run aggregate supply shifts to the right.

35. What happens in the short run when fiscal policy makers decide to increase government spending by $200 billion and reduce taxes by $200 billion?

    (A) There is no impact on the economy.
    (B) GDP increases by $200 billion.
    (C) Interest rates increase.
    (D) Tax rates have to be increased.
    (E) The government creates a surplus.

36. Assume that a reserve requirement is 20% and Joe Smith deposits into a bank $10,000 that he has been hiding under his mattress. What is the effect of this demand deposit on the excess reserves of the bank and the potential effect on the money supply?

    (A) Excess reserves increase by $10,000, and the maximum increase in the potential money supply is $50,000.
    (B) Excess reserves increase by $8,000, and the maximum increase in the potential money supply is $50,000.
    (C) Excess reserves increase by $8,000, and the maximum increase in the money supply is $40,000.
    (D) Excess reserves increase by $10,000, and the maximum increase in the money supply is $40,000.
    (E) Excess reserves increase by $40,000, and the maximum increase in the money supply is $50,000.

37. Assume that a reserve requirement is 20% and Joe Smith withdraws $10,000 from his demand deposit account at the bank. What is the effect of this demand deposit removal on the excess reserves of the bank and the effect on the potential money supply?

    (A) Excess reserves decrease by $10,000, and the maximum decrease in potential money supply is $50,000.
    (B) Excess reserves decrease by $8,000, and the maximum decrease in potential money supply is $50,000.
    (C) Excess reserves decrease by $8,000, and the maximum decrease in money potential supply is $40,000.
    (D) Excess reserves decrease by $10,000, and the maximum decrease in money potential supply is $40,000.
    (E) Excess reserves decrease by $40,000, and the maximum decrease in money potential supply is $50,000.

38. Rational self-interest

    (A) dictates that individuals with the same information will make identical choices
    (B) means that people are completely selfish
    (C) explains why people give money to charitable organizations
    (D) means that people choose options that they think will give others the smallest amount of satisfaction
    (E) is the basis for the fallacy of composition

39. What is the term for the payment for capital in the factor market?

    (A) Rent
    (B) Wage
    (C) Interest
    (D) Profit
    (E) Loss

40. In the PPF model the curve is bowed outward to indicate

    (A) gains from trade
    (B) diminishing marginal utility
    (C) diminishing returns
    (D) increasing gains from specialization
    (E) an equal trade-off ratio between two alternative goods

41. A new chip design reduces the power needed to run a computer and increases its speed and memory. What effect does this innovation have on the economy?

    (A) Increases the cost of a computer.
    (B) Shifts the PPF curve inward.
    (C) Shifts the PPF curve outward.
    (D) Has no effect.
    (E) Decreases aggregate supply.

Use the following table to answer **Questions 42 and 43**.

Production Level	Food Units	Shelter Units
A	0	200
B	10	180
C	20	140
D	30	80
E	40	0

42. If an economy is producing at level C, the cost of 10 additional units of food is

    (A) 20 shelter units
    (B) decreasing at a faster rate
    (C) 60 units of shelter
    (D) the best solution for this society
    (E) 10 food units

43. If the economy is producing 20 food units and 80 shelter units, it is

    (A) using its resources efficiently
    (B) using its resources inefficiently
    (C) producing outside the PPF curve
    (D) gaining production units
    (E) experiencing unexpected growth

Use the following table to answer **Questions 44–46**.

Production Level	Watchovria		Assertia	
	Computers	Corn	Computers	Corn
A	0	200	0	300
B	25	150	25	225
C	50	100	50	150
D	75	50	75	75
E	100	0	100	0

44. The opportunity cost in Watchovria of one unit of corn is _____ computers and in Assertia it is _____ computers.

   (A) ½, ⅓
   (B) 25, 25
   (C) ⅓, ½
   (D) 25, 50
   (E) 25, 75

45. The appropriate specialization and trade outcome are best summarized as which of the following?

   (A) Both nations are self-sufficient.
   (B) Watchovria has a comparative advantage in computers.
   (C) Assertia has a comparative advantage in computers.
   (D) If Assertia produces computers and Watchovria grows corn, both nations benefit.
   (E) Both nations should produce at the C level and trade their surpluses.

46. If Watchovria produces computers and Assertia produces corn, what terms of trade do the nations most likely require?

   (A) Watchovria trades 1 computer for 1 unit of corn.
   (B) Assertia trades 3 units of corn for 1 computer.
   (C) Watchovria trades 1 computer for more than 3 units of corn.
   (D) Assertia trades 6 units of corn for fewer than 2 computers.
   (E) Watchovria trades 1 computer for more than 2 units of corn.

47. _____and _____ economists believe that in the long run economies perform at the equilibrium level of the natural rate of unemployment.

    (A) Keynesian, monetarist
    (B) Monetarist, neoclassical
    (C) Classical, neoclassical
    (D) Keynesian, neoclassical
    (E) Monetarist, classical

48. Which of the following occurs if the government imposes a price ceiling below the equilibrium price of a good?

    (A) The quantity supplied is greater than the quantity demanded.
    (B) The firms producing this good shut down.
    (C) The quantity demanded exceeds the quantity supplied.
    (D) The price is greater than the marginal cost of the last unit produced.
    (E) If demand is perfectly elastic, profits increase for firms.

49. If the U.S. experiences an unexpected sharp increase in energy prices, the most likely result is a

    (A) rise in unemployment accompanied by a decrease in price level
    (B) shift of the short-run Phillips curve to the right
    (C) decrease in unemployment accompanied by an increase in price level
    (D) shift of the long-run Phillips curve to the left
    (E) shift of the short-run Phillips curve to the left

50. Assuming an exchange rate of $1 to 8 yuan, if the Chinese government increases its consumption of U.S. Treasury bonds, the initial impact is

    (A) depreciation of the U.S. dollar
    (B) appreciation of the U.S. dollar
    (C) appreciation of the U.S. dollar and a decrease in imports
    (D) a decrease in the export of Chinese goods
    (E) a sharp increase in unemployment in China

51. To determine the velocity of money, an economist applies which of the following formulas?

    (A) M2/Reserve ratio requirement
    (B) 1/MPS
    (C) 1/Reserve ratio requirement
    (D) Nominal GDP/Real GDP
    (E) Nominal GDP/Money supply

52. Assuming a floating currency exchange, if the FOMC decides to sell bonds in the open market, what impact does that decision have on the U.S. dollar value and exports?

	Dollar Value	Exports
(A)	Appreciate	Decrease
(B)	Depreciate	Decrease
(C)	Appreciate	Increase
(D)	Depreciate	Increase
(E)	Depreciate	No change

53. Assuming a floating currency exchange, if the FOMC decides to buy bonds in the open market, what impact does that decision have on the U.S. dollar value and exports?

	Dollar Value	Exports
(A)	Appreciate	Decrease
(B)	Depreciate	Decrease
(C)	Appreciate	Increase
(D)	Depreciate	Increase
(E)	Depreciate	No change

54. If consumer spending is $2,400 and disposable income is $3,000, the MPC and multiplier are which of the following?

	MPC	Multiplier
(A)	0.9	10
(B)	0.8	5
(C)	0.7	3.33
(D)	0.6	0.4
(E)	0.6	2.5

55. If the United States is experiencing a mild recession, which of the following could worsen it?

    (A) Congress balances the fiscal budget.
    (B) Congress cuts taxes, and the FOMC buys bonds in the open market.
    (C) Congress increases spending, and the FOMC lowers the federal funds rate.
    (D) Congress decreases bond sales, and the FOMC raises the federal funds rate.
    (E) Congress raises tariffs on foreign goods and imposes import quotas.

56. Select the best explanation for the changes in the economy depicted in the following economic model.

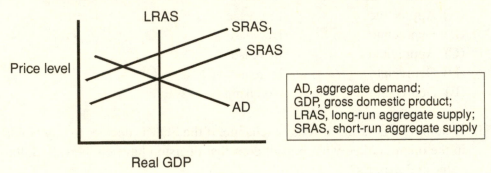

    (A) Government spending increased.
    (B) Resource input prices fell.
    (C) Exports increased.
    (D) Income taxes increased.
    (E) Resource input prices increased.

57. Assume that a hypothetical economy with an MPC of 0.8 is experiencing severe recession. By how much does government spending have to increase to shift the aggregate demand curve to the right by $25 billion?

    (A) $5 billion
    (B) $25 billion
    (C) $3.125 billion
    (D) $12.5 billion
    (E) $20 million

58. Assume that a hypothetical economy with an MPC of 0.8 is experiencing severe recession. By how much does government taxation have to decrease to shift the aggregate demand curve to the right by $25 billion?

    (A) $5 billion
    (B) $6.25 billion
    (C) $12.5 billion
    (D) $28 billion
    (E) $25 billion

59. Which of the following is NOT a function of the Federal Reserve?

    (A) Overseeing the Federal Deposit Insurance Corporation (FDIC)
    (B) Issuing Federal Reserve notes, the paper currency used in the U.S. monetary system
    (C) Setting reserve requirements and holding the reserves of banks and thrifts
    (D) Acting as the fiscal agent for the federal government
    (E) Setting monetary policy and controlling the money supply

60. Money exhibits all the following characteristics EXCEPT

    (A) it is an asset and can be used as a store of value
    (B) it must be acceptable in exchange
    (C) it is also a unit of account
    (D) any central bank can create it
    (E) without it, trade cannot occur

61. M2, the main measurement of the nation's money supply, includes all the following EXCEPT

    (A) demand deposits
    (B) all printed currency and coin
    (C) savings accounts
    (D) money market funds with values less than $100,000
    (E) money market funds with values more than $100,000

62. An unfavorable supply shock, such as an increase in gasoline prices, is most likely to have which of the following combinations of short-run effects on output and price level?

	Output	Price Level
(A)	No effect	Decrease
(B)	Increase	Decrease
(C)	Increase	Increase
(D)	Decrease	Increase
(E)	No effect	No effect

63. Under which of the following conditions is consumer spending most likely to increase?

(A) Consumers have large unpaid balances on their credit cards.
(B) Consumers' wealth is increased by changes in the stock market.
(C) The government encourages consumers to increase their savings.
(D) Social Security taxes are increased.
(E) Consumers believe they will not receive pay increases next year.

64. An increase in which of the following increases aggregate demand?

(A) Taxes
(B) Government spending
(C) Federal funds rate
(D) Reserve requirements
(E) Discount rate

65. The aggregate demand curve is downward sloping because as the price level decreases, the

(A) purchasing power increases
(B) demand for imports decreases
(C) demand for interest-sensitive expenditures increases
(D) demand for domestically produced substitute goods increases
(E) real value of fixed assets increases

66. The short-run aggregate supply curve is upward sloping because as the price level increases, the

    (A) aggregate demand for exports rises
    (B) higher cost of increased supply is covered
    (C) unemployment rate increases
    (D) real national income falls
    (E) real interest rate decreases

67. According to the circular flow model of economic activity, which of the following is not considered a leakage?

    (A) Consumer savings
    (B) Exports
    (C) Imports
    (D) Taxes
    (E) Business savings

Use the following economic model to answer **Questions 68–70**.

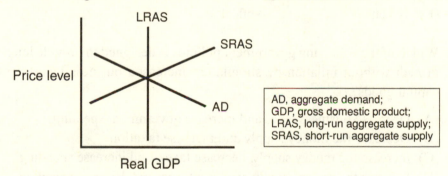

68. Assume that the economy is at full-employment equilibrium. Select the event that would cause the economy to experience inflation without increased unemployment.

    (A) A leftward shift of the aggregate demand curve.
    (B) A leftward shift of the short-run aggregate supply curve.
    (C) A rightward shift of the short-run aggregate supply curve.
    (D) A rightward shift of the aggregate demand curve only.
    (E) A rightward shift in both the short-run aggregate supply curve and the aggregate demand curve.

69. Assume that the economy is at full-employment equilibrium. Select the event that would cause the economy to experience both inflation and increased unemployment.

    (A) A leftward shift of the aggregate demand curve.
    (B) A leftward shift of the short-run aggregate supply curve.
    (C) A rightward shift of the short-run aggregate supply curve.
    (D) A rightward shift of the aggregate demand curve only.
    (E) A rightward shift in both the short-run aggregate supply curve and the aggregate demand curve.

70. Assume that the economy is at less-than-full-employment equilibrium. Select the result of increased government spending.

	Output	**Price Level**
(A)	No effect	Decrease
(B)	Increase	Decrease
(C)	Increase	Increase
(D)	Decrease	Increase
(E)	No effect	No effect

71. Which of the following government policies is designed to provide long-run growth without inflation by stimulating increased business investment in capital goods?

    (A) Decrease business taxes and increase government spending
    (B) Decrease the money supply and increase taxation
    (C) Increase the money supply, decrease taxes, and increase spending
    (D) Increase the money supply, increase taxes, and decrease spending
    (E) Increase the money supply and reduce government spending

72. If a commercial bank has no excess reserves and the reserve requirement is 20%, what is the value of new loans the bank can issue if a new customer deposits $10,000?

    (A) $10,000
    (B) $9,000
    (C) $8,000
    (D) $50,000
    (E) $1,000

73. When the Federal Reserve sells government securities in the open market, which of the following decreases in the short run?

    (A) Nominal interest rates
    (B) Nominal tax rates
    (C) Money supply
    (D) Real interest rates
    (E) Government spending

74. The federal funds rate target is the managed interest rate that is charged

    (A) to a bank's best business customers
    (B) to member banks to borrow from others banks' excess reserves overnight
    (C) and determines the Treasury yield on 30-year bonds
    (D) on all loans from the federal government
    (E) to member banks to borrow from regional banks in the Federal Reserve System

75. The discount rate is the managed interest rate charged

    (A) to a bank's best business customers
    (B) to member banks to borrow from other banks' excess reserves overnight
    (C) and determines the Treasury yield on 30-year bonds
    (D) on all loans from the federal government
    (E) to member banks to borrow from regional banks in the Federal Reserve System

76. Assume investment demand in the United States decreases and the real interest rate falls. In this situation the most likely change in the money supply (M1) in the United States and in the international value of the dollar would be which of the following?

	Money Supply	**Dollar Value**
(A)	Increase	Decrease
(B)	Decrease	Decrease
(C)	Decrease	Increase
(D)	No change	Increase
(E)	No change	Decrease

77. If the Federal Reserve pursues a policy to maintain price stability in the face of a supply shock, which of the following is most likely to increase in the short run?

    (A) Employment
    (B) Unemployment
    (C) Tax revenues
    (D) Investment
    (E) Price levels

78. If the Federal Reserve pursues a policy to increase employment in the face of a supply shock, which of the following is most likely to increase in the short run?

    (A) Employment
    (B) Unemployment
    (C) Tax revenues
    (D) Investment
    (E) Price levels

79. Assume the supply of loanable funds in country Zeta decreases. The international currency value and the exports of Zeta would react in which of the following ways?

	Currency Value	Exports
(A)	Increase	Increase
(B)	Increase	Decrease
(C)	No change	Increase
(D)	No change	Decrease
(E)	Decrease	No Change

80. Assume that investors' forward outlook causes them to sell their stocks and hold their money. What is the short-run impact on demand in the money market?

    (A) Increase
    (B) Decrease
    (C) No change
    (D) Increase in money supply
    (E) Decrease in money supply

PRACTICE TEST 2

Answer Key

1. (B)	28. (B)	55. (E)
2. (A)	29. (B)	56. (E)
3. (E)	30. (D)	57. (A)
4. (C)	31. (B)	58. (B)
5. (B)	32. (D)	59. (A)
6. (D)	33. (B)	60. (E)
7. (E)	34. (C)	61. (E)
8. (E)	35. (C)	62. (D)
9. (B)	36. (B)	63. (B)
10. (D)	37. (B)	64. (B)
11. (A)	38. (A)	65. (A)
12. (D)	39. (C)	66. (A)
13. (A)	40. (C)	67. (B)
14. (A)	41. (C)	68. (D)
15. (D)	42. (C)	69. (B)
16. (B)	43. (B)	70. (C)
17. (D)	44. (A)	71. (E)
18. (B)	45. (B)	72. (C)
19. (E)	46. (E)	73. (C)
20. (D)	47. (C)	74. (B)
21. (B)	48. (C)	75. (E)
22. (E)	49. (B)	76. (E)
23. (C)	50. (B)	77. (B)
24. (B)	51. (E)	78. (E)
25. (E)	52. (A)	79. (B)
26. (C)	53. (D)	80. (A)
27. (A)	54. (B)	

PRACTICE TEST 2
Detailed Explanations of Answers

1. **(B)**   Scarcity is the result of limited resources relative to human wants and needs.

2. **(A)**   The four factors of production, also referred to as resource inputs, are the source of household income and have an associated payment, as depicted in the circular flow model.

3. **(E)**   Productive (supply) and allocative (societal demand) efficiency drives the free-market system. Both are driven by self-interest. In the case of suppliers of goods and services, productive efficiency allows them to maintain the lowest cost that results in maximization of profit.

4. **(C)**   All resource inputs are not equal as they are exhausted. The first unit sacrificed has the greatest rate of return.

5. **(B)**   This is the basis for cost-benefit analysis. In other words, what do you have to give up to see the movie?

6. **(D)**   As you engage in trade-offs (invest more resource inputs), you find that the gain in output lessens. Therefore, as output decreases, cost rises. The marginal cost curve is the supply curve of the producer.

7. **(E)**   Calculating the percentage of change in two years from a price index requires subtracting the initial year from the current year and dividing the remainder by the initial index value. Thus, $(120 - 110)/110 = 0.09 = 9\%$.

8. **(E)**   If you chose (B), you forgot that an increase in the labor force shifts the PPF curve outward and causes underutilization of resources, thus putting production inside the curve.

9. **(B)**   Banks primarily make money by loaning money at interest rates higher than the rates they pay on deposits. They maintain cash reserves to cover demand deposit withdrawals and, of course, the Federal Reserve requirement.

10. **(D)**   The more of something you have, the less you value it. This is the law that governs demand behavior.

11. **(A)**   This is the definition of structural unemployment.

12. **(D)** Banks earn profits on the interest rate spread, but they do so at the risk of inflation rising over the time of the loan. Thus, if banks loan money at a 5% premium and inflation is unexpectedly higher, say 10%, they suffer losses.

13. **(A)** The natural rate of unemployment (NRU) is structural and frictional— types of unemployment that are not constant. For example, a technology change might result in a short-run increase in structural unemployment, leading to an increase in the NRU for that period.

14. **(A)** Consumption is one of the elements of gross domestic product, along with private investment, government spending, and net exports; therefore, GDP = C + Ig + G + Xn.

15. **(D)** GDP is the final retail sales value of all goods and services produced within a country, regardless of the national origin of the ownership. Items produced outside the borders are not included in GDP.

16. **(B)** Productivity moves the aggregate supply curve for a nation rightward. This represents an increase in real output at a lower cost-price ratio and would represent a higher standard of living.

17. **(D)** As the supply of bonds increases, their price falls, thus raising their interest yield. This higher yield increases the quantity demanded by investors, who transfer their money to the FOMC. The decrease in the money supply raises nominal interest rates and decreases investment. Since investment is a component of aggregate demand, it too decreases. This is contractionary monetary policy.

18. **(B)** The spending multiplier is 1/MPS; therefore, 1/0.40 = 2.5.

19. **(E)** Government deficits are funded by the sale of bonds. The increased supply causes bond prices to fall and yields to rise. As investors are attracted to the higher returns, they withdraw their money from banks. The decreased supply of loanable funds causes higher interest rates, and higher rates cause investment to decrease. In other words, as government demand for money increases, interest rates rise (crowding out businesses); however, if the Federal Reserve buys those bonds, the money supply increases, offsetting the otherwise higher price of money.

20. **(D)** If a currency depreciates, foreign resources (like energy) become more costly; this cost-push situation is represented by a leftward shift of aggregate supply curve. At the same time goods and services are cheaper to foreigners and exports rise, thus increasing aggregate demand. The net effect is inflationary.

21. **(B)** If a currency appreciates, the prices of goods and services are higher and exports drop. At the same time, the prices of foreign goods and services are lower, causing imports to rise.

22. **(E)** The haircut is the purchase of a final service. None of the others are final purchases, and illegal activities like the teacher's are never included in GDP.

23. **(C)** Real GDP is adjusted by the Consumer Price Index and the Personal Consumption Expenditure Index.

24. **(B)** If the money supply increases, nominal interest rates in the money market fall. This encourages banks to be more liberal in their loan policies because the cost of money to them drops and thus real interest rates fall. Investment demand quantity increases, causing real output in the long run to increase.

25. **(E)** This is another crowding-out scenario. The demand for money in the loanable funds market increases, driving interest rates higher. Investment decreases, reducing the growth rate of the economy.

26. **(C)** The higher interest rate attracts foreign investment, causing an increase in capital inflow. Foreign investors' demand for dollars causes the dollar to appreciate. The price of U.S. goods increases, causing exports to decrease, imports to rise, and net exports to decrease.

27. **(A)** This is demand-pull inflation because the economy is at full employment with no additional output possible. The injection of more money into this economy stimulates aggregate demand and results in hyperinflation.

28. **(B)** This is a contraction in the money supply. The interest rates attract foreign investment, and the dollar appreciates, causing exports to fall.

29. **(B)** The Federal Reserve has the power to contract the money supply by increasing interest rates, causing the same outcome as described in explanation 28.

30. **(D)** The total budget was $10 in 2004 and $16 in 2005. The change in prices was 6/10, or a 60% increase.

31. **(B)** This is an expansionary monetary policy. The resulting increase in the money supply lowers interest rates, causing a capital outflow. Because the international value of the dollar depreciates, exports rise as foreigners find goods are less expensive.

32. **(D)** The GDP deflator is an adjustment to nominal GDP for a change in the price level. Nominal GDP of $400 billion is multiplied by the deflator of 0.8 to get real GDP of $320 billion (in constant dollars).

33. **(B)** The injection of government spending is subject to the full multiplier. The multiplier is $1/(1 - MPC)$, or $1/MPS$, or $1/0.25 = 4$. The initial increase in spending $10 \times 4 = \$40$ billion added to GDP.

34. **(C)** Government spending is subject to the full multiplier, whereas taxes are first reduced by a reduction in the MPS. This is termed the balanced budget factor of 1, because the net injection is always equal to the initial spending amount, or in this case $200 billion. Government spending of $100 billion coupled with a tax of $100 billion results in an injection of $100 billion. Because government spending is a component of aggregate demand, the increase shifts the aggregate demand curve to the right. This is an expansionary event.

35. **(C)** The result is an increase in the size of the deficit that requires an increased sale of bonds. The increase in the supply lowers the price, driving yields and thus interest rates higher as the demand for money to buy the bonds increases. This again is a crowding-out scenario.

36. **(B)** The bank must meet the reserve requirement by securing $2,000 of the $10,000 deposit. Its loanable excess reserves are $8,000. The money multiplier (1/Reserve ratio) is 5, and the final increase is $50,000: $10,000 + (5 × $8,000).

37. **(B)** This a reverse scenario where a multiple credit contraction occurs as banks' excess reserves are reduced at a multiplied rate. Repayment of loans has the same net effect on the loanable funds of banks.

38. **(A)** Rational expectations theory, a key element of the neoclassical school of economic thought, is based on the tenet that when people receive economic information they act in a uniform manner that reflects their best self-interest. This renders fiscal and monetary policies ineffective in the long run.

39. **(C)** A simple definition of the payment for the use of the resource input known as money capital is the interest you pay.

40. **(C)** This reflects the unequal trade-off that exists between resource inputs, just as a good baker is likely to be a terrible shoemaker. As resource inputs become exhausted, they are less effective in output production.

41. **(C)** This an example of how a technology change that results in greater productivity shifts the possible combination of goods outward, symbolizing economic growth.

42. **(C)** This is a calculation of opportunity cost, what is given up to increase food production. Going from production level C to production level D, an

increase of 10 food units, requires a change in shelter units from 140 to 80, or 60 units of shelter. The 60 units of shelter is the opportunity cost or trade-off.

43. **(B)** Any combination of resources that does not represent maximum output places production outside the curve and represents an inefficient use of all resources.

44. **(A)** This is a comparative advantage calculation (opportunity cost) that also establishes the terms of trade for Watchovria. The cost to Watchovria of 1 unit of corn is half a computer (from E to D, 25 computers are lost and 50 units of corn gained; 25/50 = ½).

45. **(B)** Assertia must sacrifice 3 units of corn for 1 computer, whereas to Watchovria the cost of one computer is only 2 units of corn. Therefore, Watchovria is the least-cost producer of computers and has the comparative advantage in that product.

46. **(E)** The terms of trade must reflect the trade-off in the domestic production ratio, which for Watchovria is 1 computer to 2 units of corn and for Assertia is 3 units of corn to 1 computer. If they choose to specialize in computer production, the two countries will want to obtain a return greater than what they would receive if they did all production themselves. So Watchovria will want to trade 1 computer for more than 2 units of corn, and Assertia will want to "pay" less than 3 units of corn. So the final terms of trade are 1 computer for more than 2 but fewer than 3 units of corn.

47. **(C)** Classical and neoclassical economic theories have in common a view of the long-run aggregate supply curve as being perfectly inelastic at the natural rate of unemployment. In the short run an economy can operate above or below that limit, but market forces always move to equilibrium at full employment. This also renders the Phillips curve as perfectly inelastic in the long run as well. Even Milton Friedman (a monetarist) argued that monetary policy should focus on inflation because it cannot alter the NRU at the macro level. Altering the NRU would only be possible at the micro level.

48. **(C)** The price cap (drawn as a horizontal line below equilibrium) intersects the supply at a lower level of output and at the same time intersects demand at a higher level of output. Thus, the quantity supplied is less than the quantity demanded, creating a shortage.

49. **(B)** As discussed in explanation 47, there is only a trade-off between inflation and unemployment in the short run. Therefore, the short-run Phillips curve shifts to the right, resulting in simultaneous inflation and increased unemployment. This is a cost-push inflation scenario.

50. **(B)** The Chinese government must buy dollars to purchase the bonds, so the demand for dollars increases. The international price of the dollar appreciates as a result of this transaction.

51. **(E)** Nominal GDP, which is the total amount of money spent by society, divided by the money supply results in the rate at which those dollars are turned over (spent money, income, respent money).

52. **(A)** When the FOMC sells bonds, the money supply decreases because interest rates rise and become more attractive to foreign investors and the international value of the dollar increases. The price of U.S. goods increases to foreigners, causing exports to decrease.

53. **(D)** The sequence of events in this case is the opposite of that described in explanation 52.

54. **(B)** The MPS is the change in spending divided by the change in income: $2,400/$3,000 = 0.8. The multiplier is $1/(1 - \text{MPS})$, or $1/0.2 = 5$.

55. **(E)** All the other actions are either stimulatory or neutral. Tariffs and import quotas increase the price of goods and reduce the aggregate supply (perhaps even touching off a trade war). This worsens the recession, as these events did during the Great Depression.

56. **(E)** This is supply shock or cost-push inflation.

57. **(A)** With a multiplier of 5 ($1/0.2$) government must increase spending by $5 billion to inject $25 billion into the aggregate demand.

58. **(B)** Consumers save a portion of any tax cut based on the MPS, so 0.8 of the tax reduction is spent while 0.2 is saved and not subject to the multiplier ($1/0.2 = 5$). Thus, $0.8x = 5$, and $x = 5/0.8 = 6.25$. A tax cut of $6.25 billion would increase aggregate demand by $25 billion.

59. **(A)** The FDIC was created by an act of Congress (Glass-Steagall Act of 1933) during the Great Depression as a government agency separate from the Federal Reserve.

60. **(E)** A barter system is possible without money.

61. **(E)** Money market funds with values greater than $100,000 are not included in M2 but in the recently discontinued money measure of M3.

62. **(D)** Supply shock (as depicted in the graph for question 56) causes output to decrease and price levels to rise, resulting in stagflation.

63. **(B)** One of the main determinants of consumer spending is the "wealth effect." Even though consumers' incomes have not risen, they feel richer and so spend more.

64. **(B)** Government spending is one of the four components of aggregate demand, so an increase in spending increases aggregate demand.

65. **(A)** When price levels fall, goods and services are cheaper and thus the quantity demanded increases. The law of diminishing marginal utility governs aggregate demand.

66. **(A)** The aggregate supply curve represents the sum of all supply curves. Producer costs (marginal) rise as more is produced (law of diminishing marginal returns).

67. **(B)** Exports represent domestic production of goods and services purchased by foreigners and are measured in GDP as income flow.

68. **(D)** When the aggregate demand curve shifts rightward, the economy experiences hyperinflation of a demand-pull nature. No jobs are lost and output does not fall, but prices rise significantly.

69. **(B)** This is a stagflation scenario (as depicted in the graph for question 56) in which inflation and unemployment both increase.

70. **(C)** Government spending is an injection and shifts the aggregate demand curve rightward. Both output and employment increase. Price levels increase as resource inputs are increasingly consumed (as in wage inflation).

71. **(E)** An increase in the money supply lowers interest rates, causing increased investment and long-run economic growth. A reduction in government spending offsets the increased injection from investment and prevents the aggregate demand curve from shifting rightward, thereby causing inflation.

72. **(C)** The bank's reserve requirement is 20% of \$10,000 = \$2,000. It can lend its excess reserves beyond that amount, giving it \$8,000 in loanable funds.

73. **(C)** When the Federal Reserve sells bonds, banks that purchase those bonds have their excess reserves reduced by that amount, decreasing the money supply available in the economy and raising interest rates.

74. **(B)** The federal funds rate is the rate charged to member banks to borrow overnight from other banks' excess reserves. Banks are not allowed to violate their required reserve mandate.

75. **(E)** The president of a regional Federal Reserve Bank can request a "discount rate" from the Federal Reserve's board of governors. That is the rate the Federal Reserve charges member banks for funds and differs from the federal funds rate in that it does not apply to overnight loans.

76. **(E)** A decrease in investment demands leaves the money supply unchanged but causes interest rates to fall. The lower interest rates decrease the demand by foreigners for U.S. currency because lower yields deter foreigners from investing in U.S. financial assets.

77. **(B)** In the short run, when aggregate supply contracts (again, see the graph for question 56) inflation and unemployment result. A contractionary monetary policy (tight money) in this environment prevents further price increases but reduces investment demand and stifles any increase in aggregate demand or even shifts the curve inward, causing price levels to fall at the expense of even more jobs lost (disinflation or deflation). In the long run, however, inflation ends and employment increases as investment returns because the risk of inflation is reduced.

78. **(E)** Given the explanation for question 77, if the Federal Reserve acts in an expansionary manner by setting an easy money policy (lowering the federal funds rate), aggregate demand increases at a time when the cost of production is rising. This is the economic equivalent to pouring gas on an open flame. Price levels skyrocket, and capital flight stifles economic growth, thereby prolonging and deepening a recession.

79. **(B)** When the supply of loanable funds decreases, interest rates rise. Higher interest rates attract foreign investment to these financial assets, the international demand for dollars increases, domestic goods become more expensive in foreign currency, and exports fall.

80. **(A)** The immediate effect of the sale of stock is an increased demand for money by the purchaser of that asset. This increased demand for money causes interest rates on loanable funds to increase. The stock of money does not change because money changed hands and was neither created nor destroyed.

ANSWER SHEETS

Practice Test 1
Practice Test 2

PRACTICE TEST 1

Answer Sheet

1. Ⓐ Ⓑ Ⓒ Ⓓ Ⓔ	28. Ⓐ Ⓑ Ⓒ Ⓓ Ⓔ	55. Ⓐ Ⓑ Ⓒ Ⓓ Ⓔ
2. Ⓐ Ⓑ Ⓒ Ⓓ Ⓔ	29. Ⓐ Ⓑ Ⓒ Ⓓ Ⓔ	56. Ⓐ Ⓑ Ⓒ Ⓓ Ⓔ
3. Ⓐ Ⓑ Ⓒ Ⓓ Ⓔ	30. Ⓐ Ⓑ Ⓒ Ⓓ Ⓔ	57. Ⓐ Ⓑ Ⓒ Ⓓ Ⓔ
4. Ⓐ Ⓑ Ⓒ Ⓓ Ⓔ	31. Ⓐ Ⓑ Ⓒ Ⓓ Ⓔ	58. Ⓐ Ⓑ Ⓒ Ⓓ Ⓔ
5. Ⓐ Ⓑ Ⓒ Ⓓ Ⓔ	32. Ⓐ Ⓑ Ⓒ Ⓓ Ⓔ	59. Ⓐ Ⓑ Ⓒ Ⓓ Ⓔ
6. Ⓐ Ⓑ Ⓒ Ⓓ Ⓔ	33. Ⓐ Ⓑ Ⓒ Ⓓ Ⓔ	60. Ⓐ Ⓑ Ⓒ Ⓓ Ⓔ
7. Ⓐ Ⓑ Ⓒ Ⓓ Ⓔ	34. Ⓐ Ⓑ Ⓒ Ⓓ Ⓔ	61. Ⓐ Ⓑ Ⓒ Ⓓ Ⓔ
8. Ⓐ Ⓑ Ⓒ Ⓓ Ⓔ	35. Ⓐ Ⓑ Ⓒ Ⓓ Ⓔ	62. Ⓐ Ⓑ Ⓒ Ⓓ Ⓔ
9. Ⓐ Ⓑ Ⓒ Ⓓ Ⓔ	36. Ⓐ Ⓑ Ⓒ Ⓓ Ⓔ	63. Ⓐ Ⓑ Ⓒ Ⓓ Ⓔ
10. Ⓐ Ⓑ Ⓒ Ⓓ Ⓔ	37. Ⓐ Ⓑ Ⓒ Ⓓ Ⓔ	64. Ⓐ Ⓑ Ⓒ Ⓓ Ⓔ
11. Ⓐ Ⓑ Ⓒ Ⓓ Ⓔ	38. Ⓐ Ⓑ Ⓒ Ⓓ Ⓔ	65. Ⓐ Ⓑ Ⓒ Ⓓ Ⓔ
12. Ⓐ Ⓑ Ⓒ Ⓓ Ⓔ	39. Ⓐ Ⓑ Ⓒ Ⓓ Ⓔ	66. Ⓐ Ⓑ Ⓒ Ⓓ Ⓔ
13. Ⓐ Ⓑ Ⓒ Ⓓ Ⓔ	40. Ⓐ Ⓑ Ⓒ Ⓓ Ⓔ	67. Ⓐ Ⓑ Ⓒ Ⓓ Ⓔ
14. Ⓐ Ⓑ Ⓒ Ⓓ Ⓔ	41. Ⓐ Ⓑ Ⓒ Ⓓ Ⓔ	68. Ⓐ Ⓑ Ⓒ Ⓓ Ⓔ
15. Ⓐ Ⓑ Ⓒ Ⓓ Ⓔ	42. Ⓐ Ⓑ Ⓒ Ⓓ Ⓔ	69. Ⓐ Ⓑ Ⓒ Ⓓ Ⓔ
16. Ⓐ Ⓑ Ⓒ Ⓓ Ⓔ	43. Ⓐ Ⓑ Ⓒ Ⓓ Ⓔ	70. Ⓐ Ⓑ Ⓒ Ⓓ Ⓔ
17. Ⓐ Ⓑ Ⓒ Ⓓ Ⓔ	44. Ⓐ Ⓑ Ⓒ Ⓓ Ⓔ	71. Ⓐ Ⓑ Ⓒ Ⓓ Ⓔ
18. Ⓐ Ⓑ Ⓒ Ⓓ Ⓔ	45. Ⓐ Ⓑ Ⓒ Ⓓ Ⓔ	72. Ⓐ Ⓑ Ⓒ Ⓓ Ⓔ
19. Ⓐ Ⓑ Ⓒ Ⓓ Ⓔ	46. Ⓐ Ⓑ Ⓒ Ⓓ Ⓔ	73. Ⓐ Ⓑ Ⓒ Ⓓ Ⓔ
20. Ⓐ Ⓑ Ⓒ Ⓓ Ⓔ	47. Ⓐ Ⓑ Ⓒ Ⓓ Ⓔ	74. Ⓐ Ⓑ Ⓒ Ⓓ Ⓔ
21. Ⓐ Ⓑ Ⓒ Ⓓ Ⓔ	48. Ⓐ Ⓑ Ⓒ Ⓓ Ⓔ	75. Ⓐ Ⓑ Ⓒ Ⓓ Ⓔ
22. Ⓐ Ⓑ Ⓒ Ⓓ Ⓔ	49. Ⓐ Ⓑ Ⓒ Ⓓ Ⓔ	76. Ⓐ Ⓑ Ⓒ Ⓓ Ⓔ
23. Ⓐ Ⓑ Ⓒ Ⓓ Ⓔ	50. Ⓐ Ⓑ Ⓒ Ⓓ Ⓔ	77. Ⓐ Ⓑ Ⓒ Ⓓ Ⓔ
24. Ⓐ Ⓑ Ⓒ Ⓓ Ⓔ	51. Ⓐ Ⓑ Ⓒ Ⓓ Ⓔ	78. Ⓐ Ⓑ Ⓒ Ⓓ Ⓔ
25. Ⓐ Ⓑ Ⓒ Ⓓ Ⓔ	52. Ⓐ Ⓑ Ⓒ Ⓓ Ⓔ	79. Ⓐ Ⓑ Ⓒ Ⓓ Ⓔ
26. Ⓐ Ⓑ Ⓒ Ⓓ Ⓔ	53. Ⓐ Ⓑ Ⓒ Ⓓ Ⓔ	80. Ⓐ Ⓑ Ⓒ Ⓓ Ⓔ
27. Ⓐ Ⓑ Ⓒ Ⓓ Ⓔ	54. Ⓐ Ⓑ Ⓒ Ⓓ Ⓔ	

PRACTICE TEST 2

Answer Sheet

1. Ⓐ Ⓑ Ⓒ Ⓓ Ⓔ
2. Ⓐ Ⓑ Ⓒ Ⓓ Ⓔ
3. Ⓐ Ⓑ Ⓒ Ⓓ Ⓔ
4. Ⓐ Ⓑ Ⓒ Ⓓ Ⓔ
5. Ⓐ Ⓑ Ⓒ Ⓓ Ⓔ
6. Ⓐ Ⓑ Ⓒ Ⓓ Ⓔ
7. Ⓐ Ⓑ Ⓒ Ⓓ Ⓔ
8. Ⓐ Ⓑ Ⓒ Ⓓ Ⓔ
9. Ⓐ Ⓑ Ⓒ Ⓓ Ⓔ
10. Ⓐ Ⓑ Ⓒ Ⓓ Ⓔ
11. Ⓐ Ⓑ Ⓒ Ⓓ Ⓔ
12. Ⓐ Ⓑ Ⓒ Ⓓ Ⓔ
13. Ⓐ Ⓑ Ⓒ Ⓓ Ⓔ
14. Ⓐ Ⓑ Ⓒ Ⓓ Ⓔ
15. Ⓐ Ⓑ Ⓒ Ⓓ Ⓔ
16. Ⓐ Ⓑ Ⓒ Ⓓ Ⓔ
17. Ⓐ Ⓑ Ⓒ Ⓓ Ⓔ
18. Ⓐ Ⓑ Ⓒ Ⓓ Ⓔ
19. Ⓐ Ⓑ Ⓒ Ⓓ Ⓔ
20. Ⓐ Ⓑ Ⓒ Ⓓ Ⓔ
21. Ⓐ Ⓑ Ⓒ Ⓓ Ⓔ
22. Ⓐ Ⓑ Ⓒ Ⓓ Ⓔ
23. Ⓐ Ⓑ Ⓒ Ⓓ Ⓔ
24. Ⓐ Ⓑ Ⓒ Ⓓ Ⓔ
25. Ⓐ Ⓑ Ⓒ Ⓓ Ⓔ
26. Ⓐ Ⓑ Ⓒ Ⓓ Ⓔ
27. Ⓐ Ⓑ Ⓒ Ⓓ Ⓔ

28. Ⓐ Ⓑ Ⓒ Ⓓ Ⓔ
29. Ⓐ Ⓑ Ⓒ Ⓓ Ⓔ
30. Ⓐ Ⓑ Ⓒ Ⓓ Ⓔ
31. Ⓐ Ⓑ Ⓒ Ⓓ Ⓔ
32. Ⓐ Ⓑ Ⓒ Ⓓ Ⓔ
33. Ⓐ Ⓑ Ⓒ Ⓓ Ⓔ
34. Ⓐ Ⓑ Ⓒ Ⓓ Ⓔ
35. Ⓐ Ⓑ Ⓒ Ⓓ Ⓔ
36. Ⓐ Ⓑ Ⓒ Ⓓ Ⓔ
37. Ⓐ Ⓑ Ⓒ Ⓓ Ⓔ
38. Ⓐ Ⓑ Ⓒ Ⓓ Ⓔ
39. Ⓐ Ⓑ Ⓒ Ⓓ Ⓔ
40. Ⓐ Ⓑ Ⓒ Ⓓ Ⓔ
41. Ⓐ Ⓑ Ⓒ Ⓓ Ⓔ
42. Ⓐ Ⓑ Ⓒ Ⓓ Ⓔ
43. Ⓐ Ⓑ Ⓒ Ⓓ Ⓔ
44. Ⓐ Ⓑ Ⓒ Ⓓ Ⓔ
45. Ⓐ Ⓑ Ⓒ Ⓓ Ⓔ
46. Ⓐ Ⓑ Ⓒ Ⓓ Ⓔ
47. Ⓐ Ⓑ Ⓒ Ⓓ Ⓔ
48. Ⓐ Ⓑ Ⓒ Ⓓ Ⓔ
49. Ⓐ Ⓑ Ⓒ Ⓓ Ⓔ
50. Ⓐ Ⓑ Ⓒ Ⓓ Ⓔ
51. Ⓐ Ⓑ Ⓒ Ⓓ Ⓔ
52. Ⓐ Ⓑ Ⓒ Ⓓ Ⓔ
53. Ⓐ Ⓑ Ⓒ Ⓓ Ⓔ
54. Ⓐ Ⓑ Ⓒ Ⓓ Ⓔ

55. Ⓐ Ⓑ Ⓒ Ⓓ Ⓔ
56. Ⓐ Ⓑ Ⓒ Ⓓ Ⓔ
57. Ⓐ Ⓑ Ⓒ Ⓓ Ⓔ
58. Ⓐ Ⓑ Ⓒ Ⓓ Ⓔ
59. Ⓐ Ⓑ Ⓒ Ⓓ Ⓔ
60. Ⓐ Ⓑ Ⓒ Ⓓ Ⓔ
61. Ⓐ Ⓑ Ⓒ Ⓓ Ⓔ
62. Ⓐ Ⓑ Ⓒ Ⓓ Ⓔ
63. Ⓐ Ⓑ Ⓒ Ⓓ Ⓔ
64. Ⓐ Ⓑ Ⓒ Ⓓ Ⓔ
65. Ⓐ Ⓑ Ⓒ Ⓓ Ⓔ
66. Ⓐ Ⓑ Ⓒ Ⓓ Ⓔ
67. Ⓐ Ⓑ Ⓒ Ⓓ Ⓔ
68. Ⓐ Ⓑ Ⓒ Ⓓ Ⓔ
69. Ⓐ Ⓑ Ⓒ Ⓓ Ⓔ
70. Ⓐ Ⓑ Ⓒ Ⓓ Ⓔ
71. Ⓐ Ⓑ Ⓒ Ⓓ Ⓔ
72. Ⓐ Ⓑ Ⓒ Ⓓ Ⓔ
73. Ⓐ Ⓑ Ⓒ Ⓓ Ⓔ
74. Ⓐ Ⓑ Ⓒ Ⓓ Ⓔ
75. Ⓐ Ⓑ Ⓒ Ⓓ Ⓔ
76. Ⓐ Ⓑ Ⓒ Ⓓ Ⓔ
77. Ⓐ Ⓑ Ⓒ Ⓓ Ⓔ
78. Ⓐ Ⓑ Ⓒ Ⓓ Ⓔ
79. Ⓐ Ⓑ Ⓒ Ⓓ Ⓔ
80. Ⓐ Ⓑ Ⓒ Ⓓ Ⓔ

Glossary

aggregate demand–shows the total quantity of goods and services consumed at different price and output levels.

aggregate demand/aggregate supply (AD/AS) model–uses aggregate demand and aggregate supply to determine and explain price level, real domestic output, disposable income, and employment.

aggregate expenditure–all spending for final goods and services in an economy: $C + I_g + G + Xn = AE$.

aggregate supply shocks–unexpected, large changes in resource costs that shift an economy's aggregate supply curve.

allocative efficiency–distribution of resources among firms and industries to obtain production quantities of the products most wanted by society (consumers); where marginal cost equals marginal benefit.

appreciation (of the dollar)–an increase in the value of the dollar relative to the currency of another nation, so that a dollar buys more of the foreign currency and thus foreign goods become cheaper; critical to long-run trade equilibrium.

asset–items of monetary value owned by a firm or individual; opposite is liability.

asset demand for money–various amounts of money people want to hold as a store of value; the amount varies inversely with the interest rate; critical to monetary policy.

average fixed cost (AFC)–firm's total fixed cost divided by output.

average product–total output produced per unit of a resource employed (total product divided by the quantity of input).

average total cost (ATC)–firm's total cost divided by output, equal to average fixed cost plus average variable cost (AFC + AVC = ATC).

average variable cost (AVC)–firm's total variable cost divided by output.

balanced-budget multiplier–extent to which an equal change in government spending and taxes changes equilibrium gross domestic product; always has a value of 1, because it is equal to the amount of the equal changes in G and T (T is subject to the MPS of consumers and spending is not).

balance sheet–statement of the assets and liabilities that determines a firm's net (solvency).

balance of payments account–the summary of a nation's current account and its financial account.

balance of trade–a nation's current account balance; net exports.

barrier to entry–artificial prevention of the entry of firms into an industry.

Board of Governors–seven-member group that supervises and controls the money and banking system; appointed by president to 14-year staggered terms; the Federal Reserve Board.

bond–financial instrument through which a borrower (corporate or government) is contracted to pay the principal at a specified interest rate at a specific date (maturity) in the future; promissory note.

break-even point–output at which a (competitive) firm's total cost and total revenue are equal (TR = TC); an output at which a firm has neither an economic profit nor a loss, at which it earns only a normal profit.

Bretton Woods system–international monetary system developed after the Second World War. Under this system, adjustable pegs were employed, the International Monetary Fund helped stabilize foreign exchange rates, and gold (gold standard set at $35 U.S. per ounce of gold) and the dollar were used as international monetary reserves.

budget deficit–amount by which the spending of the (federal) government exceeds its tax revenues in any year.

budget surplus–amount by which the tax revenues of the (federal) government exceed its spending in any year.

built-in (automatic) stabilizers–programs that react to changes in the business cycle without additional government action, increasing government's budget deficit (or reducing its surplus) during a recession and increasing government's budget surplus (or reducing its deficit) during inflation. Unemployment insurance is one such program.

business cycle–records the increases and decreases in the level of economic activity over periods of time. Consists of expansion (boom), peak, recession (bust or contraction), trough (bottom), and recovery phases. GDP data is generally used to plot this cycle, a lagging indicator.

capital–resources (buildings, machinery, and equipment) used to produce goods and services; also called investment goods.

capital account–section of a nation's international balance-of-payments balance sheet that records foreign purchases of U.S. assets (money in) and U.S. purchases of foreign assets (money out).

capital account inflow (outflow)–reflects the net difference between foreign funds invested in the home country minus the domestic funds invested in the foreign country. A component of the balance of payments account.

capitalism–free market economic system in which property is privately owned and the invisible forces of supply and demand set price and quantity.

cartel–overt agreement among firms (or countries) in an industry to fix the price of a product and establish output quotas.

central bank–government agency whose chief function is the control of the nation's money supply; the Federal Reserve.

change in demand–change in the quantity demanded of a good or service at all prices; a shift of the demand curve to the left (decrease) or right (increase).

change in supply–change in the quantity supplied of a good or service at all prices; a shift of the supply curve to the left (decrease) or right (increase).

circular flow model–flow of resource inputs from households to businesses and of g/s from businesses to households. A flow in the opposite direction of money—businesses to households for inputs and from households to businesses for g/s—occurs simultaneously.

Classical economics–school of macroeconomic generalizations accepted by most economists prior to the depression of the 1930s; a main feature was that the free market economy was self-regulating and would naturally return to full employment levels of output.

collusion–when firms act together (collude) to fix prices, divide a market, or otherwise restrict competition; illegal in the United States.

command system–economic system in which property is publicly owned (means of production) and government uses central economic planning to direct and coordinate economic activities; state-planned economy in which price and quantity are set by government (as in the former USSR).

comparative advantage–determines specialization and exchange rate for trade between nations; based on the nation with the lower relative or comparative cost of production.

competition–Adam Smith's requirement for success of a free market, a market of independent buyers and sellers competing with one another; includes ease of access to and exit from the marketplace.

complementary goods–goods that are used together, so if the price of one falls, the demand for the other decreases as well (and vice versa).

concentration ratio–a simple method of determining a monopoly, which adds the percentage of the total sales of an industry made by the four largest sellers in the industry. If the sum is greater than 50%, the industry is considered a shared monopoly.

conglomerate merger–merger of a firm in one industry with a firm in an unrelated industry.

consumer price index (CPI)–index that measures the prices of a set "basket" of some 300 g/s bought by a "typical" consumer; used by government as a main indicator of the rate of inflation.

consumer surplus–that portion of the demand curve that lies above the equilibrium price level and denotes those consumers that would be willing to buy the g/s at higher price levels.

contractionary fiscal policy–combination of government reduction in spending and a net increase in taxes, for the purpose of decreasing aggregate demand, lowering price levels, and thus controlling inflation.

corporation–legal entity ("like a person") chartered by a state or the federal government; limits liability for business debt to the assets of the firm.

cost-push inflation–when an increase in resource costs shifts the aggregate supply curve inward, resulting in an increase in the price level and unemployment; also termed *stagflation*.

cross elasticity of demand–ratio of the percentage change in quantity demanded of one good to the percentage change in the price of another good. If the coefficient is positive, the two goods are substitute. If the coefficient is negative, they are considered complementary.

crowding-out effect–caused by the federal government's increased borrowing in the money market that results in a rise in interest rates. The rise in interest rates results in a decrease in gross business domestic investment (I_g), which reduces the effectiveness of expansionary fiscal policy.

currency rate of exchange–the price in one domestic currency to purchase a unit of another nation's currency. For example, 1 U.S. dollar buys 1.50 Canadian dollars.

current account–section in a nation's international balance of payments that records its exports and imports of goods and services, its net investment income, and its net transfers. A component of the balance of payments account.

cyclical deficit–federal budget deficit caused by a recession and the resultant decline in tax revenues.

cyclical unemployment–type of unemployment caused by recession; less than full employment aggregate demand.

deadweight loss (efficiency loss)–the foregone total societal surplus associated with the levy of a tax that discourages what had heretofore been a mutually advantageous market transaction.

deflation–decline in the economy's price level; indicates contraction in business cycle or may signal expansion of total output (aggregate supply moves to the right).

demand–the quantity of a g/s that buyers wish to buy at various prices.

depreciation (of the dollar)–decrease in the value of the dollar relative to another currency, so that the dollar buys a smaller amount of the foreign currency and therefore the price of foreign goods increases; tends to reduce imports and increase exports.

derived demand–orders for a production input that depend on a demand for the product that the input helps to produce.

determinants of demand–factors other than price that alter (shift) the quantities demanded of a good or service.

determinants of supply–factors other than price that alter (shift) the quantities supplied of a good or service.

direct relationship–correlation between two variables that change in the same direction; for example, income and spending.

discount rate–interest rate that the Federal Reserve Banks charge on the loans they make to banks (different from the federal funds rate).

discretionary fiscal policy–deliberate changes in taxes (rates and types) and government spending by Congress.

disposable income–personal income minus personal taxes; income available for consumption expenditures and saving.

dissaving–when spending for consumer g/s exceeds disposable income.

dumping–predatory business practice; sale of products below cost in a foreign country or below the domestic prices.

durable good–consumer good with an expected life (use) of three or more years; decrease in sales indicates recession, as contraction affects these goods before nondurables.

easy money policy–Federal Reserve actions designed to stimulate gross business domestic investment (I_g) and thus aggregate demand; counters recession by increasing the money supply to lower interest rates and expand real GDP.

economic efficiency–use of the minimum necessary inputs to obtain the most societally beneficial quantity of g/s; employs both productive and allocative efficiency.

economic profit–total revenue of a firm minus its economic costs (both explicit and implicit costs); also termed *pure profit* and *above-normal profit*.

economic rent–price paid for the use of land and other natural resources, the supply of which is fixed.

economies of scale–savings in the average total cost of production as the firm expands the size of plant (its output) in the long run.

elastic demand–product or resource demand whose price elasticity is greater than 1. This means that the resulting percentage change in quantity demanded is greater than the percentage change in price.

elastic supply–product or resource supply whose price elasticity is greater than 1. This means that the resulting percentage change in quantity supplied is greater than the percentage change in price.

entitlement programs–government programs, such as social insurance, food stamps, Medicare, and Medicaid, that guarantee benefits to all who fit the programs' criteria.

equilibrium price–price at which the quantity demanded and the quantity supplied are equal (intersect), shelves clear, and price stability occurs.

equilibrium quantity–quantity demanded and supplied at the equilibrium price.

excess capacity–plant resources underused when imperfectly competitive firms produce less output than that associated with achieving minimum average total cost.

exchange rate–trade ratio of one nation's currency for another nation's currency.

expansionary fiscal policy–combination of government increases in spending and a net decrease in taxes, for the purpose of increasing aggregate demand, increasing output and disposable income, and lowering unemployment.

expected rate of return–profit a firm anticipates it will obtain by purchasing capital goods; influences investment demand for money.

explicit cost–payment a firm must make to an outsider to obtain a production input.

factors of production–resources: land, capital, and entrepreneurial ability.

federal funds rate–the interest rate banks and other depository institutions charge one another on overnight loans made out of their excess reserves; targeted by monetary policy.

Federal Open Market Committee (FOMC)–the 12-member group that determines the purchase and sale policies of the Federal Reserve Banks in the market for U.S. government securities; affects federal funds rate.

Federal Reserve Banks–12 banks chartered by the U.S. government to control the money supply and perform other functions such as clearing checks.

Federal Trade Commission (FTC)–commission of five members established by the Federal Trade Commission Act of 1914 to investigate unfair competitive practices of firms, to hold hearings on complaints of such practices, and to issue cease-and-desist orders when firms have been found to have engaged in such practices.

financial account (capital account)–the difference between a country's sale of assets to foreigners and its purchase of foreign assets. A component of the balance of payments.

fixed cost–any cost that remains constant when the firm changes its output.

fixed exchange rate–rate of currency exchange that is set, prevented from rising or falling with changes in currency supply and demand; opposite of floating rate.

floating exchange rate–rate of exchange determined by the international demand for and supply of a nation's money; free to increase or decrease.

frictional unemployment–unemployment caused by workers' voluntarily changing jobs or workers' being between jobs.

full employment unemployment rate–natural rate of unemployment when there is no cyclical unemployment. In the United States, equals between 4% and 5%, because some frictional and structural unemployment is unavoidable.

GDP deflator–price index found by dividing nominal GDP by real GDP; used to adjust nominal GDP to real GDP.

General Agreement on Tariffs and Trade (GATT)–international agreement, reached in 1947, in which 23 nations agreed to reduce tariff rates and eliminate import quotas. The Uruguay Round of the GATT talks led to the World Trade Organization.

government transfer payment–money (or g/s) issued to an individual by a government for which the government receives no direct payment from that person.

gross domestic product (GDP)–total market value of all final goods and services produced annually within the boundaries of the United States, whether by U.S. or foreign-supplied resources.

horizontal merger–merger into a single firm of two firms that produce the same product and sell it in the same geographic market.

hyperinflation–a very rapid rise in the price level; an extremely high rate of inflation.

imperfect competition–all market structures except pure competition; includes monopoly, monopolistic competition, and oligopoly.

implicit cost–the monetary income a firm sacrifices when it uses a resource it owns rather than supplying the resource in the market; equal to what the resource could have earned in the best-paying alternative employment; includes a normal profit.

indifference curve–curve showing the different combinations of two products that yield the same satisfaction or utility to a consumer.

inelastic demand–product or resource demand for which the elasticity coefficient for price is less than 1. This means the resulting percentage change in quantity demanded is less than the percentage change in price.

inelastic supply–product or resource supply for which the price elasticity coefficient is less than 1. The percentage change in quantity supplied is less than the percentage change in price.

inferior good–a g/s the consumption of which declines as income rises (and vice versa), with price remaining constant.

inflation–rise in the general level of prices.

inflation (rational) expectations–a key determinant that impacts the loanable funds market for both borrowers and lenders.

inflation targeting–a central bank practice that requires a predetermined, agreed-upon rate of inflation to be sought by monetary policy.

inflationary gap–amount by which the aggregate expenditure and schedule must shift downward to decrease the nominal GDP to its full employment noninflationary level.

injection–a way of viewing an increase of a component(s) of aggregate expenditure that may result in an overall increase of aggregate demand; opposite of leakage. Addition of spending such as investment, government purchases, or net exports.

interest–payment for the use of borrowed money.

intermediate goods–products purchased for resale or further processing or manufacturing.

international balance of payments–all the transactions that took place between one nation and those of all other nations during a year.

International Monetary Fund (IMF)–the international association of nations that was formed after the Second World War to make loans of foreign monies to nations with temporary payment deficits and, until the early 1970s, to administer the adjustable pegs. It now mainly makes loans to nations that face possible defaults on private and government loans.

inventories–goods that have been produced but remain unsold.

inverse relationship–the relationship between two variables that change in opposite directions; for example, product price and quantity demanded.

invisible hand–tendency of firms and resource suppliers that seek to further their own self-interests in competitive markets also to promote the interest of society as a whole.

Keynesian economics–macroeconomic generalizations leading to the conclusion that a capitalistic economy is characterized by macroeconomic instability and that fiscal policy and monetary policy can be used to promote full employment, price level stability, and economic growth.

kinked demand curve–demand curve for a noncollusive oligopolist, which is based on the assumption that rivals will follow a price decrease and ignore a price increase.

Laffer Curve–curve relating government tax rates and tax revenues and on which a particular tax rate (between 0 and 100 percent) maximizes tax revenues.

law of demand–the principle that, other things being equal, an increase in the price of a product will reduce the quantity of that product demanded, and conversely for a decrease in price.

law of diminishing marginal utility–the principle that as a consumer increases the consumption of a good or service, the marginal utility obtained from each additional unit of the g/s decreases.

law of diminishing returns–the principle that as successive increments of a variable resource are added to a fixed resource, the marginal product of the variable resource will eventually decrease.

law of increasing opportunity costs–the principle that as the production of a good increases, the opportunity cost of producing an additional unit rises.

law of supply–the principle that, other things being equal, an increase in the price of a product will increase the quantity of that product supplied, and conversely for a price decrease.

leakage–(1) a withdrawal of potential spending from the income-expenditures stream via saving, tax payments, or imports; (2) a withdrawal that reduces the lending potential of the banking system.

least-cost combination of resources–the quantity of each resource a firm must employ to produce a particular output at the lowest total cost; the combination at which the ratio of the marginal product of a resource to its marginal resource cost (to its price if the resource is employed in a competitive market) is the same for the last dollar spent on each of the resources employed.

liability–a debt with a monetary value; an amount owed by a firm or an individual.

liquidity–the ease with which an asset can be converted—quickly— into cash with little or no loss of purchasing power. Money is said to be perfectly liquid, whereas other assets have a lesser degree of liquidity.

liquidity trap–a point in an economy where the nominal interest rate is zero with the theoretical result that monetary policy would be exhausted.

loanable funds market–a conceptual market wherein the demand for money is determined by borrowers and the supply is determined by lenders. Market equilibrium prices the interest rate.

long run–time frame necessary for producers to alter resource inputs and increase

or decrease output; time frame necessary for adjustments to be made as a result of shifts in aggregate demand and supply.

Lorenz curve–a model that demonstrates the cumulative percentage of population and their cumulative share of income; used to show shifts in income distribution across population over time.

M1, M2, M3–money supply measurements that increasingly broaden the definition of money measured; critical to monetarism and interest rates.

macroeconomics–the portion of economics concerned with the overall performance of the economy; focused on aggregate demand-aggregate supply relationship, and the resultant output, income, employment, and price levels.

marginal benefit–change in total benefit that results from the consumption of one more unit of output.

marginal cost–change in total cost that results from the sale of one more unit of output.

marginal product–change in total output relative to the change in resource input.

marginal propensity to consume–change in consumption spending relative to a change in income.

marginal propensity to save–change in saving relative to a change in income.

marginal revenue–change in total revenue that results from the sale of one more unit of product.

marginal revenue cost (MRC)–change in total cost with the addition of one more unit of resource input for production.

marginal revenue product (MRP)–change in total revenue with the addition of one more unit of resource input for production.

marginal utility–the use a consumer gains from the addition of one more unit of a g/s.

market failure–the inability of the free market to provide public goods; over- or underallocation of g/s that have negative/positive externalities; used to justify government intervention.

Medicaid–entitlement program that finances medical costs for needy individuals.

Medicare–compulsory hospital insurance for the elderly, supplied by federal government through transfer payments of taxed wages.

microeconomics–portion of economics concerned with the individual elements that make up the economy: households, firms, government, and resource input prices.

monetarism–economic belief that the main cause of change in aggregate output and price level is movement in the money supply and the resultant interest rate.

monetary policy–policy basis on which the Federal Reserve influences interest rates through manipulation of the money supply to promote price stability, full employment, and productivity growth.

money–any article (paper note, metal coin) generally accepted as having value in exchange for a g/s.

money supply–defined, measured, and reported as M_1, M_2, M_3.

monopsony–a market structure in which there is only one buyer of a resource input or g/s.

MR = MC principle–law stating that to maximize profit and minimize loss, a firm will produce at the output level where the marginal revenue is equal to the marginal cost.

MRP = MRC formula–equation showing that to maximize profit and minimize loss, a firm will employ a resource input quantity when the marginal revenue product is equal to the marginal resource cost of the resource input.

multiplier–the effect that a change in one of the four components of aggregate expenditure has on GDP.

national (public) debt–money owed by the federal government to owners of government securities, equal to the total amount of money borrowed during all deficit spending.

national debt–the accumulated cyclical deficits of the Federal government over time.

natural monopoly–an industry in which the economy of scale is so large that one producer is the most efficient least-cost producer; usually regulated by government.

natural rate of unemployment–frictional and structural unemployment, the full employment rate, zero cyclical unemployment.

Neo-classical economics–recently developed school of economic thought that macroeconomic instability (recession) is always a short-run event. In the long run, the economy is stable at full employment (NRU) as prices and wages automatically adjust for downturns in GDP causing an eventual return to a full employment, noninflationary output. This renders fiscal and monetary policy ineffective in the long run due in large part to the effect of rational expectations.

net export effect–any monetary or fiscal policy action is magnified (+ or –) by the effect that the change in U.S. dollar value (interest rates effect exchange rates) has on import and export prices.

normal good–a g/s the consumption of which increases as income increases (opposite of inferior g/s).

normal profit–where price equals average total cost, and cost includes the implicit cost of entrepreneurial value.

North American Free Trade Agreement (NAFTA)–1993 trade agreement between Canada, the United States, and Mexico, designed to reduce trade barriers over a 15-year period.

natural rate of unemployment–a fluctuating rate determined by adding frictional to structural unemployment. It is equal to the long-run aggregate supply.

"nominal"–any economic measurement that is unadjusted for inflation.

nominal interest rate–the interest rate unadjusted for inflation

oligopoly–a market structure in which a few firms have a large market share and sell differentiated products. In oligopolies, firms tend to have large economies of scale, pricing is mutually dependent, and price wars can occur; there is a kinked-demand curve.

Organization of Petroleum Exporting Countries (OPEC)–a cartel that has control of about 60% of the world's oil and has at times effected severe price change by limiting production quotas.

partnership–an unincorporated firm with shared ownership.

PCE index–an inflation measurement indicator that includes current goods and services consumption, chain linked to their prior year's price.

perfectly elastic demand–infinite quantity demanded at a particular price; graphed as a straight horizontal line.

perfectly elastic supply–infinite quantity supplied at a particular price; graphed as a straight horizontal line.

perfectly inelastic demand–quantity demanded does not change in response to a change in price; graphed as a vertical straight line.

perfectly inelastic supply–quantity supplied does not change in response to a change in price; graphed as a horizontal straight line.

Phillips Curve (short-run)–a model that demonstrates the inverse relationship between unemployment (horizontal) and inflation (vertical axis).

Phillips Curve (long-run)–a model that demonstrates that after inflation expectations have been adjusted, there is no trade off between inflation and unemployment, as it is vertical and equal to the NRU.

policy mix–recognition that fiscal and monetary policies are not independent and that in some circumstances are a necessary complement to each other.

price–the sum of money necessary to purchase a g/s.

Price = MC–in a purely competitive market model, the principle that a firm's demand is perfectly elastic and equal to price, so that a firm will maximize profit when price equals marginal cost if price is equal to or greater than ATC and minimize loss if price is greater than AVC.

price ceiling–a price set below equilibrium by government.

price elasticity of demand–percentage of change in quantity demanded divided by percentage of change in price; measures responsiveness to price changes.

price elasticity of supply–percentage of change in quantity supplied divided by percentage of change in price; measures responsiveness to price changes.

price fixing–illegal collusion between producers to set an above-equilibrium price.

price floor–a price set above equilibrium by government.

producer surplus–that portion of the supply curve that lies below equilibrium price and denotes producers that would bring the g/s to market at even lower prices.

progressive tax–a marginal tax rate system in which the percentage of tax increases as income increases and vice versa (such as U.S. federal income tax brackets).

proportional tax–a flat tax system in which the percentage of tax remains fixed as income changes.

public good–a g/s provided by government for which price does not exclude use and use is indivisible into individual components.

pure competition–market structure in which so many firms produce a very similar g/s that no firm has significant control over market price; a "price taker."

pure monopoly–market structure in which one firm is the sole producer of a distinct g/s and thus has significant control over market price; a "price maker."

quantity demanded–various amounts along a consumer demand curve showing the quantity consumers will buy at various prices.

quantity supplied–various amounts along a producer supply curve showing the quantity producers will sell at various prices.

"rational expectations"–a key component of the neo classical economic viewpoint that simply states that as monetary/fiscal policy attempts to alter economic outcomes, people anticipate and adjust their behaviors, thereby mitigating the effects. Thus, in the long run, there is always a return to the natural rate of unemployment.

"real"–an economic measurement (such as GDP or income) that has been adjusted for inflation.

real interest rate–the interest rate adjusted for inflation.

recession–two consecutive business quarters of negative real GDP.

regressive tax–a set tax percentage the average rate of which decreases as the taxpayer's income increases, and vice versa; an example is sales tax.

required reserve ratio–a legally fixed percentage of a bank's reserves (demand deposits) that must be deposited with a Federal Reserve Bank.

Say's Law–a controversial generalization that the production of goods and services creates an equal demand for those g/s. Associated with economic policies under President Reagan.

shortage–difference between the quantity demanded of a g/s and the quantity supplied at a below-equilibrium price ($Q_d > Q_s$).

short run–the length of time during which a producer is unable to alter all the inputs of production.

shut-down point–point at which a firm will cease production because revenue would fall below average variable cost.

sole proprietorship–an unincorporated business owned by an individual.

specialization–concentration of resource(s) in the production of a g/s that results in increased efficiency of production.

spillover benefit–positive externality. Production or consumption results in benefits (such as education) not intended by the market participants.

spillover cost–negative externality. Production or consumption results in costs (such as pollution) not borne by the market participants.

stock–an ownership share in a company held by an investor.

structural unemployment–unemployment resulting from a mismatch of worker skill to demand or location.

subsidy–government financial support for which no direct payment is collected.

substitute–goods or services that are interchangeable. When the price of one increases, the demand for the other increases.

supply-side economics–macroeconomic perspective that emphasizes fiscal policies aimed at altering the state of the economy through I_g (short run) and the aggregate supply (long run).

surplus–difference between the quantity demanded of a g/s and the quantity supplied at an above-equilibrium price ($Q_d < Q_s$).

tariff–a tax on imports/exports.

tax–a required payment of money to government, for which the payer receives no direct g/s.

tight money policy–policy basis on which the Federal Reserve System acts to contract the money supply and increase interest rates, thereby slowing the economy.

trade deficit–amount by which a nation's imports exceed its exports.

trade-off–forgone alternative use of a resource in the production of a g/s.

trade surplus–amount by which a nation's exports exceed its imports.

variable cost–cost of inputs that fluctuates as a firm increases or decreases its output.

World Bank–organization that lends to developing nations to assist them in achieving economic growth.

World Trade Organization (WTO)–group established by the Uruguay Round of the GATT to assist in the promotion of trade and resolution of trade disputes.

Index

Notes